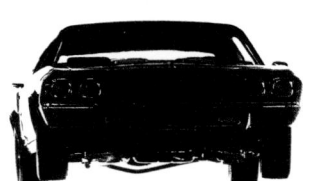

A BOOK OF FLYING CARS

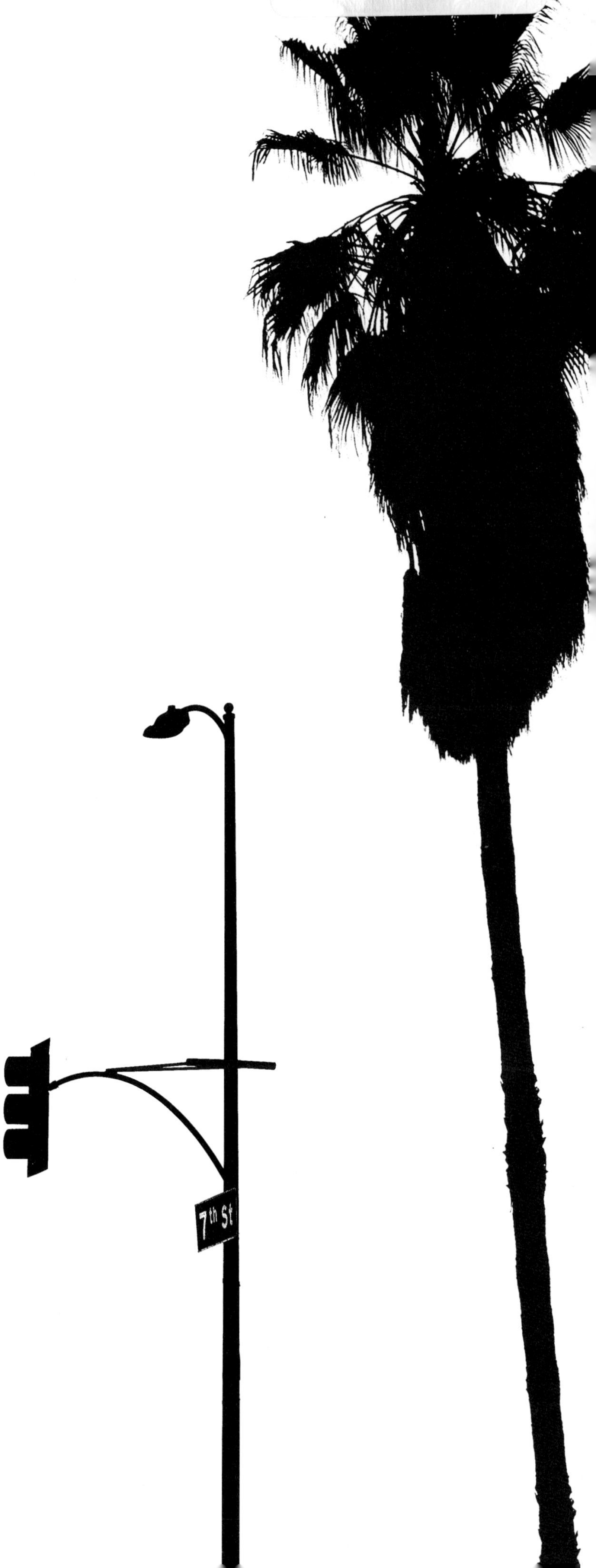

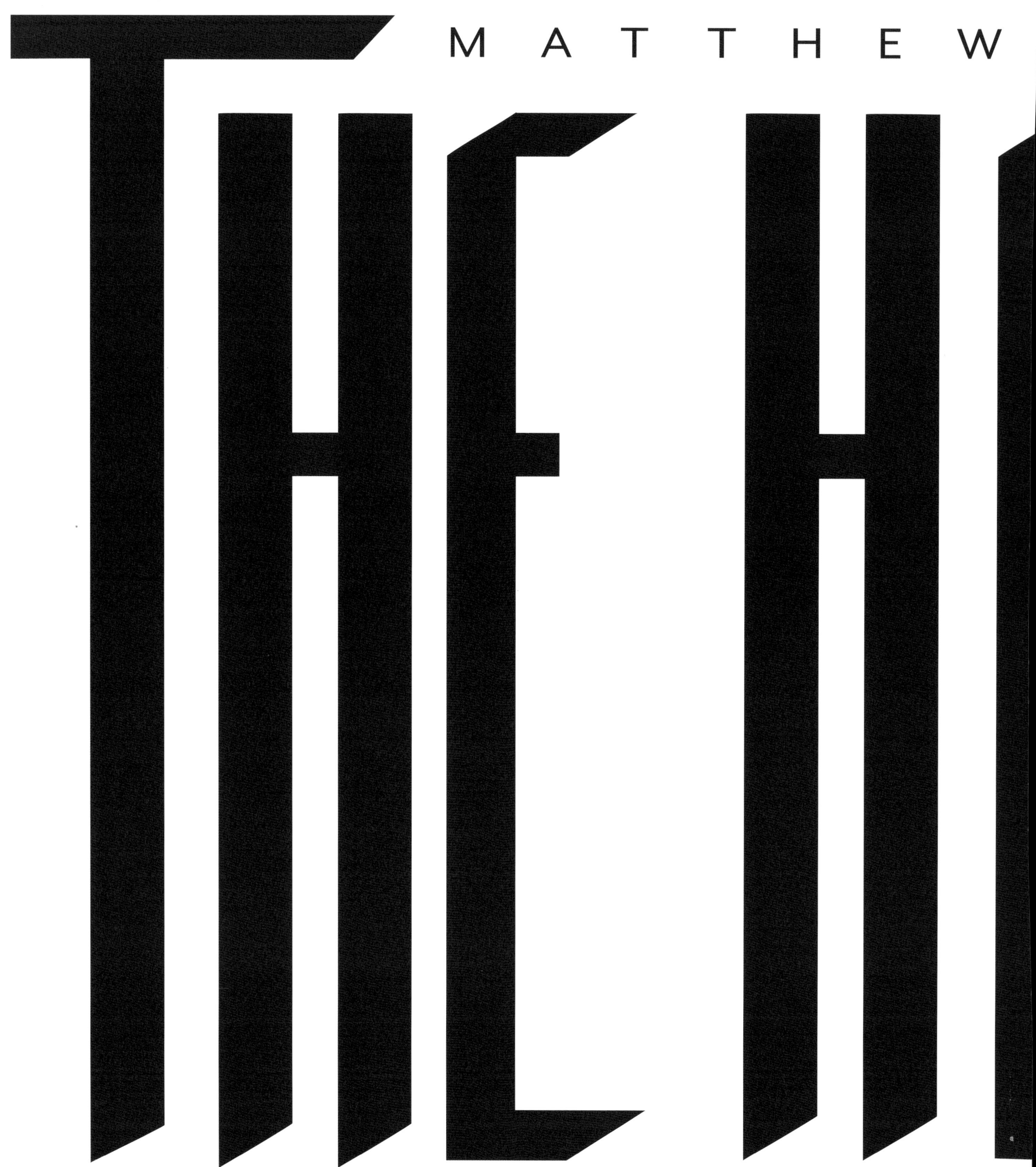

PORTER FIGHTS

aperture

OVERSHOT

2005

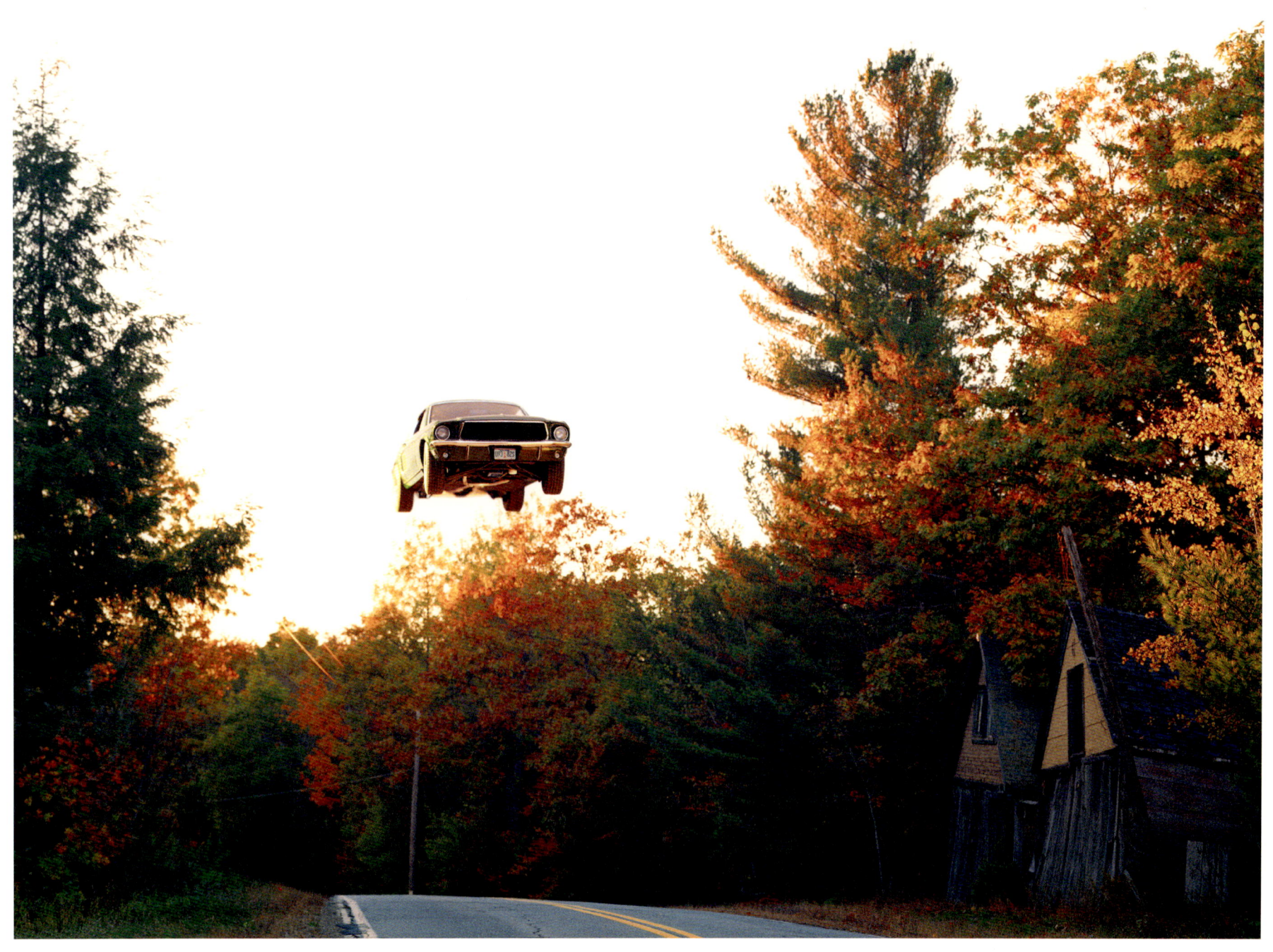

Gone in 60 Sentences

Rachel Kushner

Every time I've attempted to start this sidewinding meditation on Matthew Porter's airborne muscle cars, cars that are things and also backlit silhouettes of things, I end up scrolling the new version of the old Autotrader, online, and looking at models of cars I've always wanted and haven't yet owned, and also their silhouettes.

If I had a hundred grand to drop right now, this morning, which I don't, I could buy a 1969 GTO Judge, mint. But really it's not my style. A '67 GTO and its classy cigar-box lines is what I always wanted. The '69 is a novelty item, like roller skates or a leather shirt, and anyhow I get bored of the color orange. I'd love a GTO but I don't need a Judge, even if there are certain days—Tuesdays?—when I feel like I need a Judge.

For a Sunday drive I want a Stutz Blackhawk; doesn't even have to be the one Elvis owned. I'll humbly accept some other Stutz, but the more I research who owned Stutzes—Dean Martin, Wilson Pickett, George Foreman, Muhammad Ali, Willie Nelson, and Barry White, just to cherry-pick from the longer list of celebrity owners—I get mad that I haven't yet myself acquired the pink slip for a Stutz. Even if I could afford one, there aren't very many, and today none are listed for sale.

There's a 1965 Mercury Marauder, I always liked those. Even if the lines are a little square, the fastback makes up for it, although it's a car that has to have sport rims or forget it.

Why is 1965 the chicane through which all American car design went from curved to boxy?

Nineteen sixty-eight was another chicane, that led to puffy quarter panels, and even outright blimpage.

Sometimes I start to believe I want a Rolls-Royce, like a model from the 1980s. Today you can buy a 1985 Rolls-Royce Silver Spur for ten grand on Autotrader. I know nothing about Rolls models but if it doesn't come with pull-down teakwood dinner trays in the backseat the deal is off. Extras are important to me. The idea of a General Motors Lanvin Arpège perfume atomizer offered stock with the 1958 Cadillac Eldorado Brougham spritzes my spirit with something American that I can actually, for a moment, believe in.

I often want a 1961 Ford Starliner. That's something special to me, and it harkens back to one I saw for sale in Napa, California, in 1992. It was Wimbledon White, a stock Ford color I'm partial to. I didn't buy it. Say it: Starliner. Wimbledon White. That was the year I spent every weekend looking at cars. I ended up buying a 1964 Ford Galaxie, which I still own, but even after I bought my Galaxie I continued combing PennySaver and Autotrader and Hemmings and called numbers and dreamed of other cars. In 1997 I bought a 1963 Chevrolet Impala in Hendersonville, North Carolina. The night I bought it, a friend and I motored out to a drive-in movie theater in Waynesville, North Carolina. We could hear cows lowing as we waited for the film to begin. Wish I still had that car. Had to sell it to pay for school, made a very large profit since it's a coveted year of a coveted model. The night before I sold it someone attempted to steal it from my parents' driveway in San Francisco. My neighbors saw my car in the middle of the street and knocked on our door. A guy had hot-wired it and was planning to drive away with the anti-theft club still attached to the wheel. He flooded the engine trying to give it gas and had to abandon it on foot.

It's September as I write this, and the 2018 calendar my son got at the Pomona car show is turned to a 1971 Mustang Boss 351. I've seen every muscle car a hundred times over. That was youth. This is now (middle age). I've given my copy of the *Standard Catalog of American Cars, 1946–1975* to my son, who can pore over specs like I once did. The '71 Mustang is shown parked in front of a tacky Italianate villa. The parked car versus the midair car is object instead of subject. A car flying through an intersection is the protagonist; that's clear. It knows the story and it is the story, even if the casual grace of electric wires, light poles, and traffic signals play their parts. Nothing like late-day light to put the city-sky infrastructure into relief: the light is half the charm of these magical images. The locations that Porter has chosen, too, are sweet, but maybe in part because they're familiar: some of them are in my neighborhood, or near it. He doesn't photograph famously steep Baxter Street in Echo Park, but his images conjure it. Cresting Baxter to get air is something LAPD motorcycle cops do at five a.m., when they figure no one is paying attention. They hit Baxter Street and court broken axles.

There are many iconic cinema stills of flying muscle cars, but the mother lode of the genre is from H. B. Halicki's 1974 film *Gone in 60 Seconds*, in which a Mustang Mach I hovers midair in a Los Angeles intersection after launching off a crash-pile it has used as a jump ramp.

The film's super-flimsy plotline involves the theft of forty-eight cars in forty-eight hours, each coded with a woman's name. The Mach I, called "Eleanor," is the indisputable star and credited as such. Halicki financed, produced, directed, wrote, starred in, and did all of the stunt driving for the film. He was known as the Car Crash King, and he was also the Junkyard King, who owned all ninety-three of the cars that were totaled in his movie, including multiple police cars, fire trucks, and even the garbage truck that drives right over a Dodge Charger. In my favorite scene, Eleanor the Mach I plows into a large sofa that's sitting in the middle of an alleyway, the sofa compressed and pulverized as the car commits to dragging the ruined frame of the couch from its undercarriage for several hundred feet.

The parked car versus the midair car is object instead of subject. A car flying through an intersection is the protagonist; that's clear. It knows the story and it is the story, even if the casual grace of electric wires, light poles, and traffic signals play their parts.

There are other comical touches. Halicki evades police in a tow truck with a rear-facing Dodge Challenger, a mint car that later gets shoved in a compactor at a wrecking yard. Cornered at one point after a high-speed pursuit in the Mach I, Halicki seems to assent to the police, as if the game is over. He puts his hands up at officers' commands, multiple guns drawn on him from various angles. He keeps his hands up, but mashes the gas with his driving foot, complying and not complying, hands kept up as he blazes west on Ocean Boulevard and cops dive out of the way.

In other highlights, Eleanor the Mach I runs over a shopping cart full of groceries. A night scene at the long-gone Ascot Park speedway reveals the inspiration for the film's title, a message for speedway guests to lock their vehicles or they'll be "gone in sixty seconds." A high-speed chase interrupts the Carson City Council's dedication of a new sherriff's department, a scene I favor because Carson is where, coincidentally, the best go-karting in Los Angeles can be had—or rather, the most scrappy and sketchy go-karting in Los Angeles. Another highlight is when Eleanor drives right into a Cadillac dealership, escaping through the service department.

But the heart of the film is a long and static sequence in a huge garage, as the camera slow-pans past every one of the forty-eight stolen vehicles, Rolls-Royces and Cadillacs and Lincolns, a Plymouth Barracuda, a Corvette Stingray, a Manta Mirage, car after car, some rare, some not, all gleaming and still. They are part of the plot but real—actual cars that Halicki owned (and which, in real life, he'd acquired dubiously). A woman named Pumpkin sits behind a desk, the superego in the room, leaning back. She has big hair, I mean really big—amazing hair, and long nails. The studs on the collar of her denim shirt wink at the camera, her Malibu-tan hands tented in rumination, although maybe she's thinking only of money, or of nothing at all. Either way, I love her. Her name is Marion Busia and apparently she is now, as you read this, a real estate agent in Rancho Palos Verdes. This is not disappointing. I'd settle for nothing less.

Joined to the theme of destroying cars is a fetish for cars, but also other stuff. Halicki's belt buckles are different in every scene, and never subtle. He's got a lot of sunglasses, bell-bottoms, and briefcases. Several wigs and an artificial mustache. Various styles of slim jim, for opening car doors. An array of hats and deerskin driving gloves. He was a collector. I heard he later acquired his own Goodyear Blimp but I'm having trouble verifying that.

H. B. Halicki died while filming a sequel to *Gone in 60 Seconds*. A telephone pole was clipped by a wire meant to pull a water tower into a parking lot full of cars, and the telephone pole hit Halicki and killed him.

Time passes. People die. They become real estate agents. Car collections get auctioned. Classics become more valuable, and rarer, and also forgotten, and thus, to some, less valuable, and that's good, and also sad. The light stays the same. Or rather, it is always changing.

BOROUGH PRIME

2015

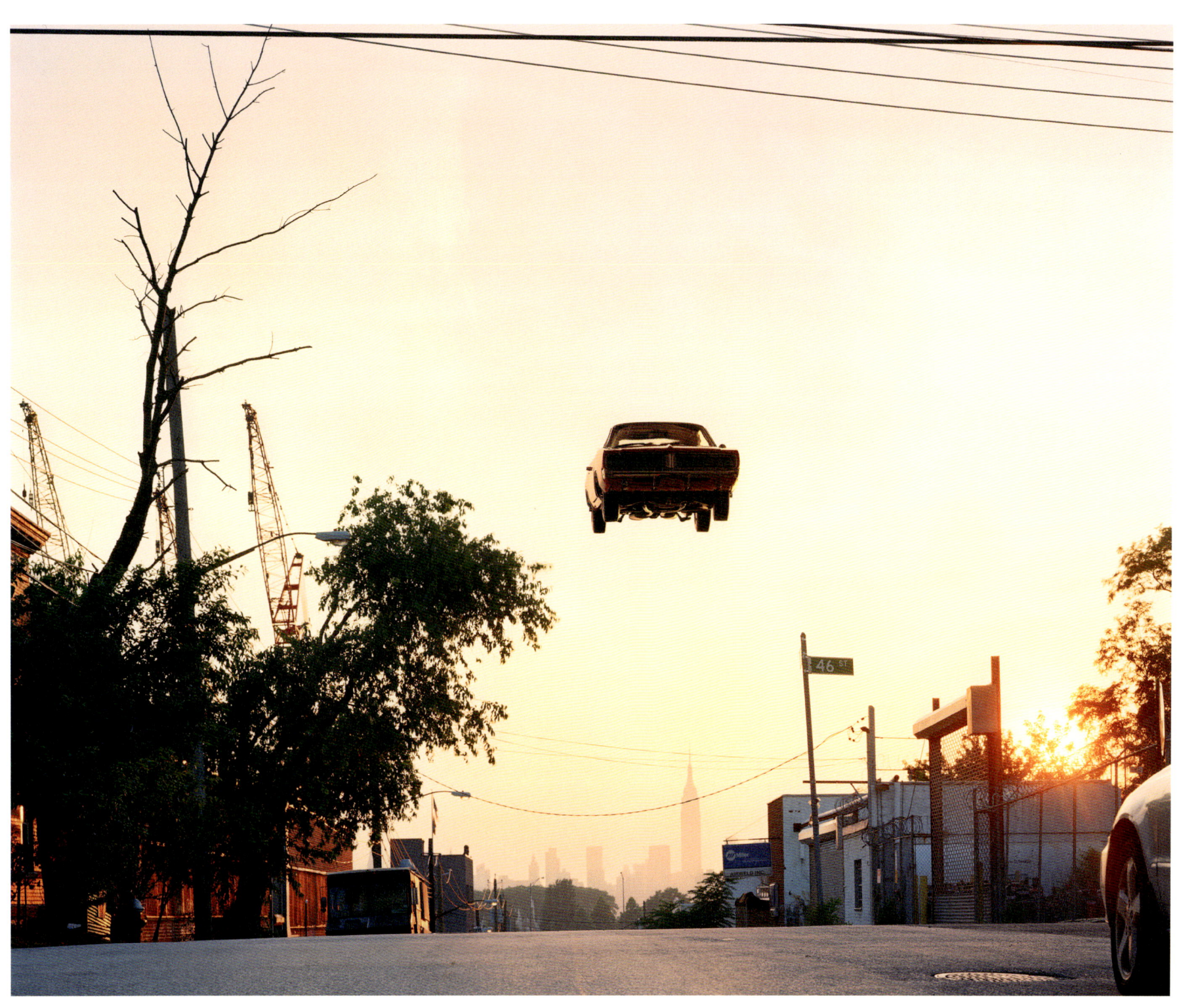

SUTRO TOWER

2011

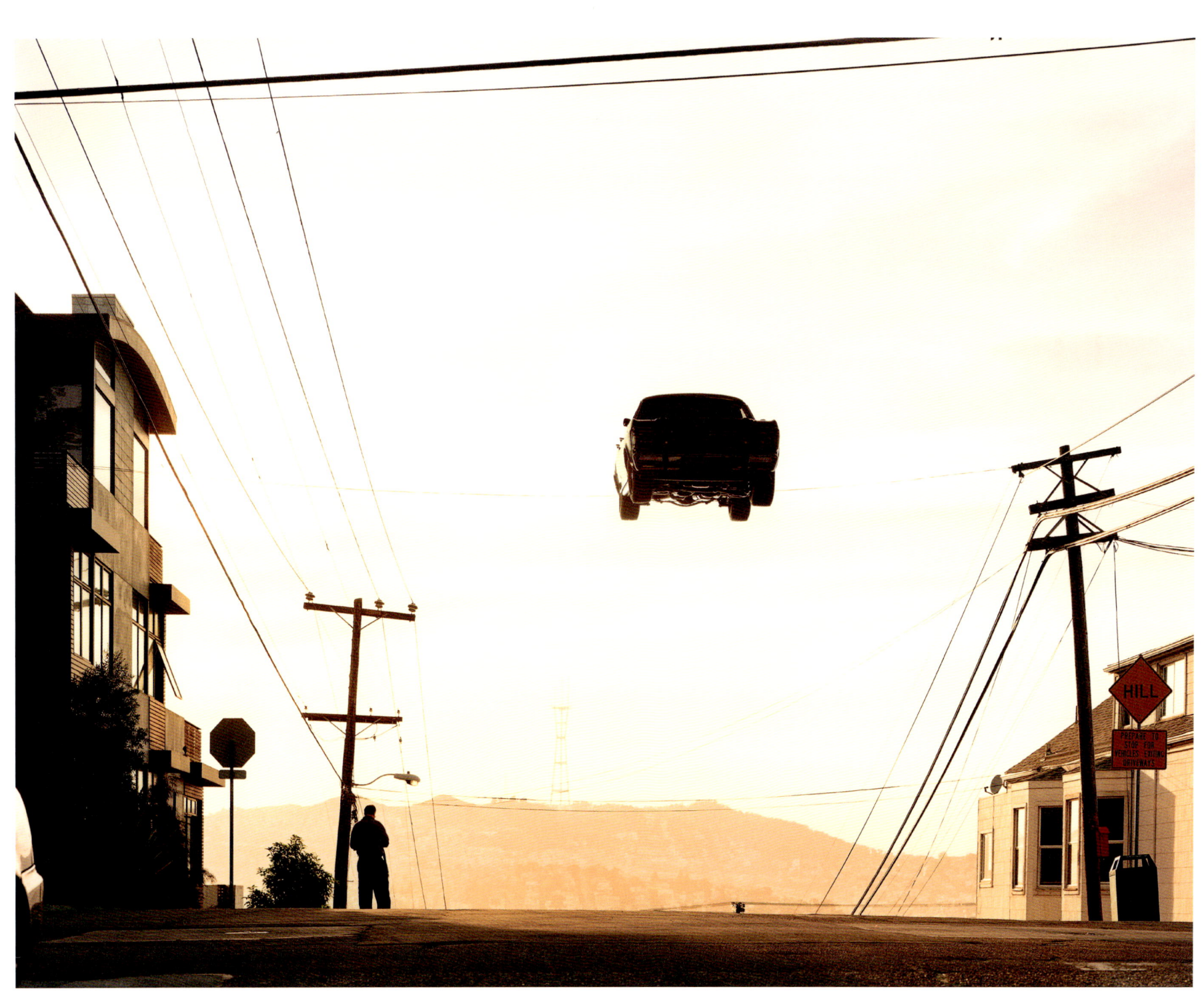

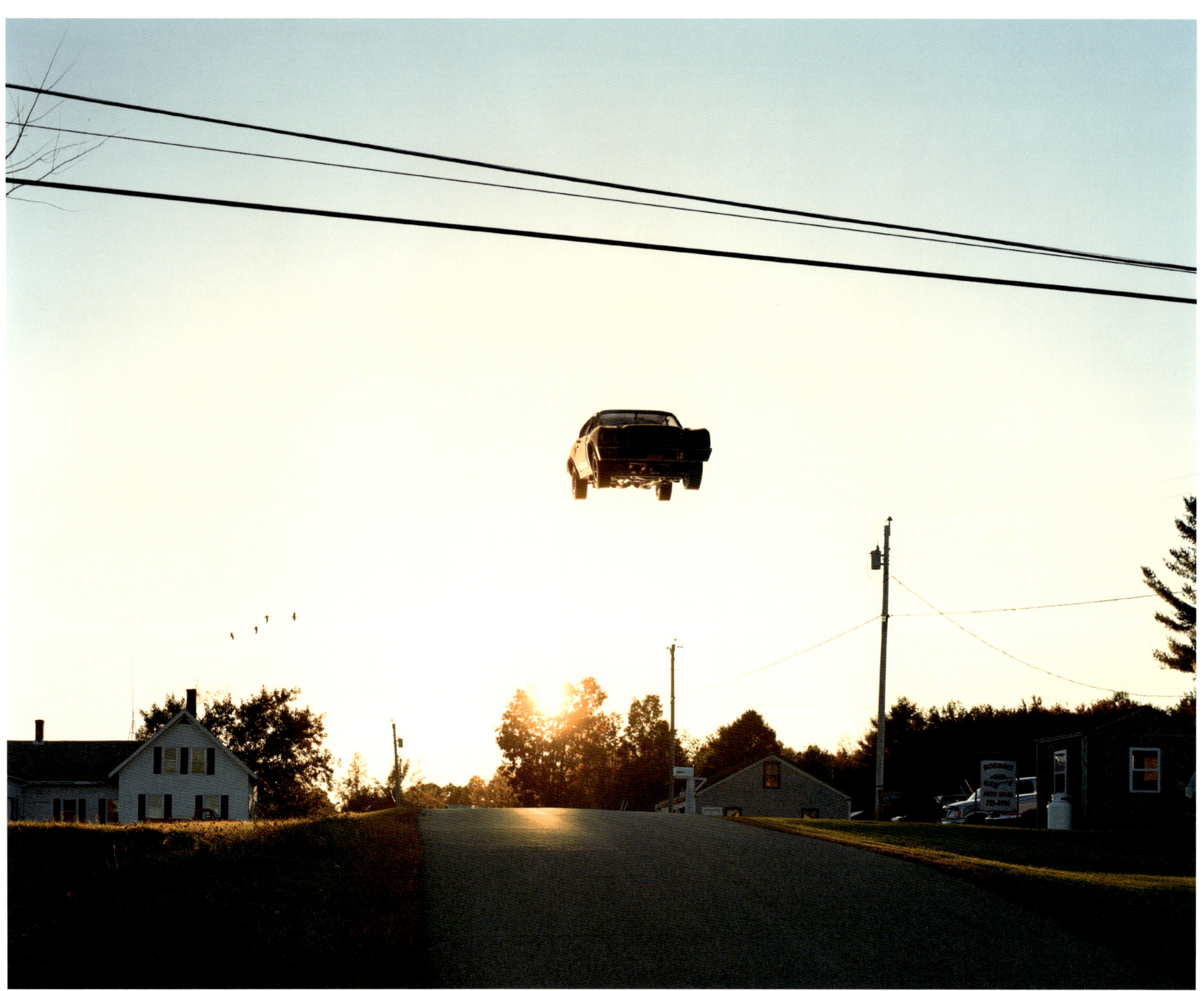

UPSTATE
2014

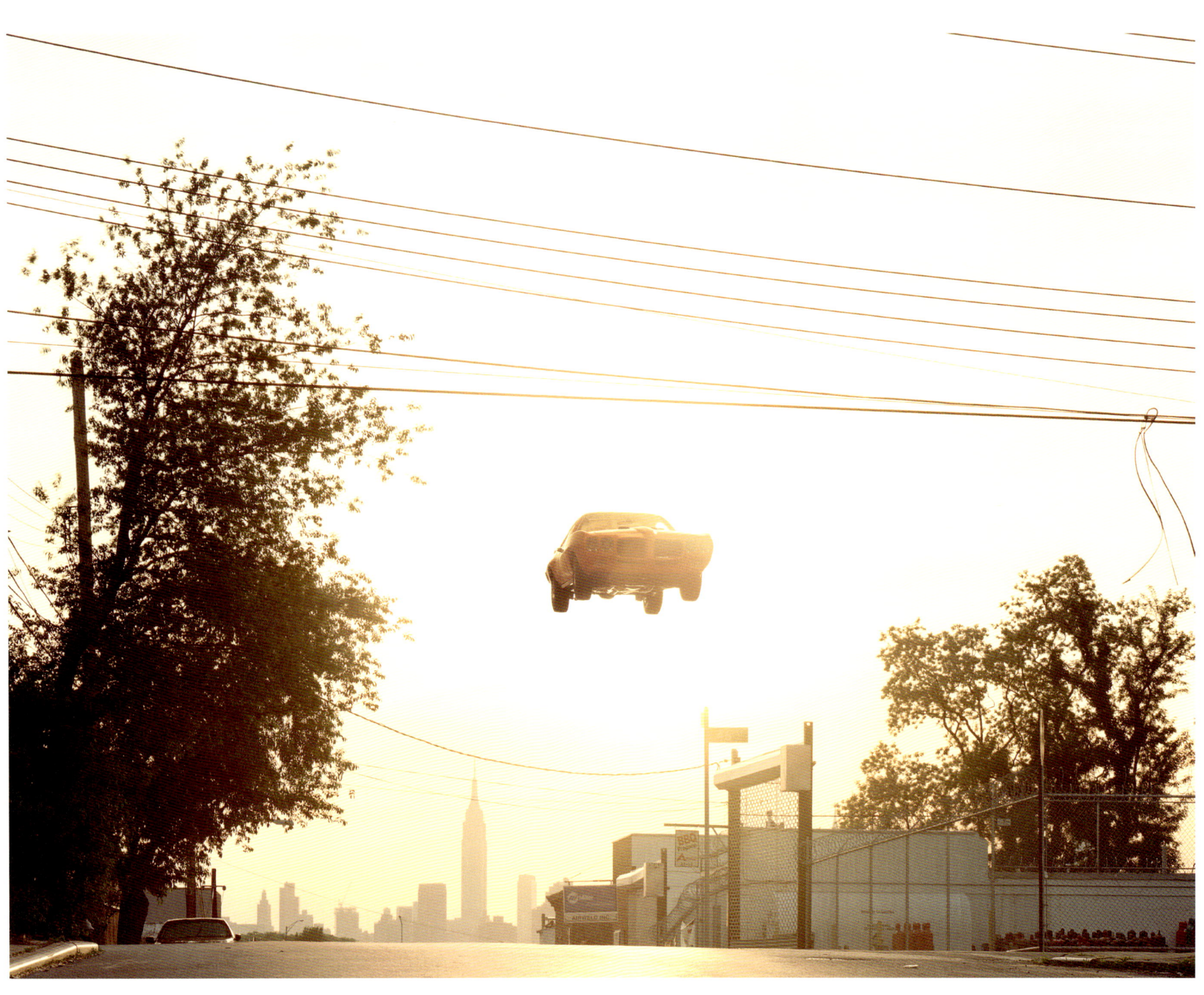

EMPIRE

2010

BAYVIEW
2006

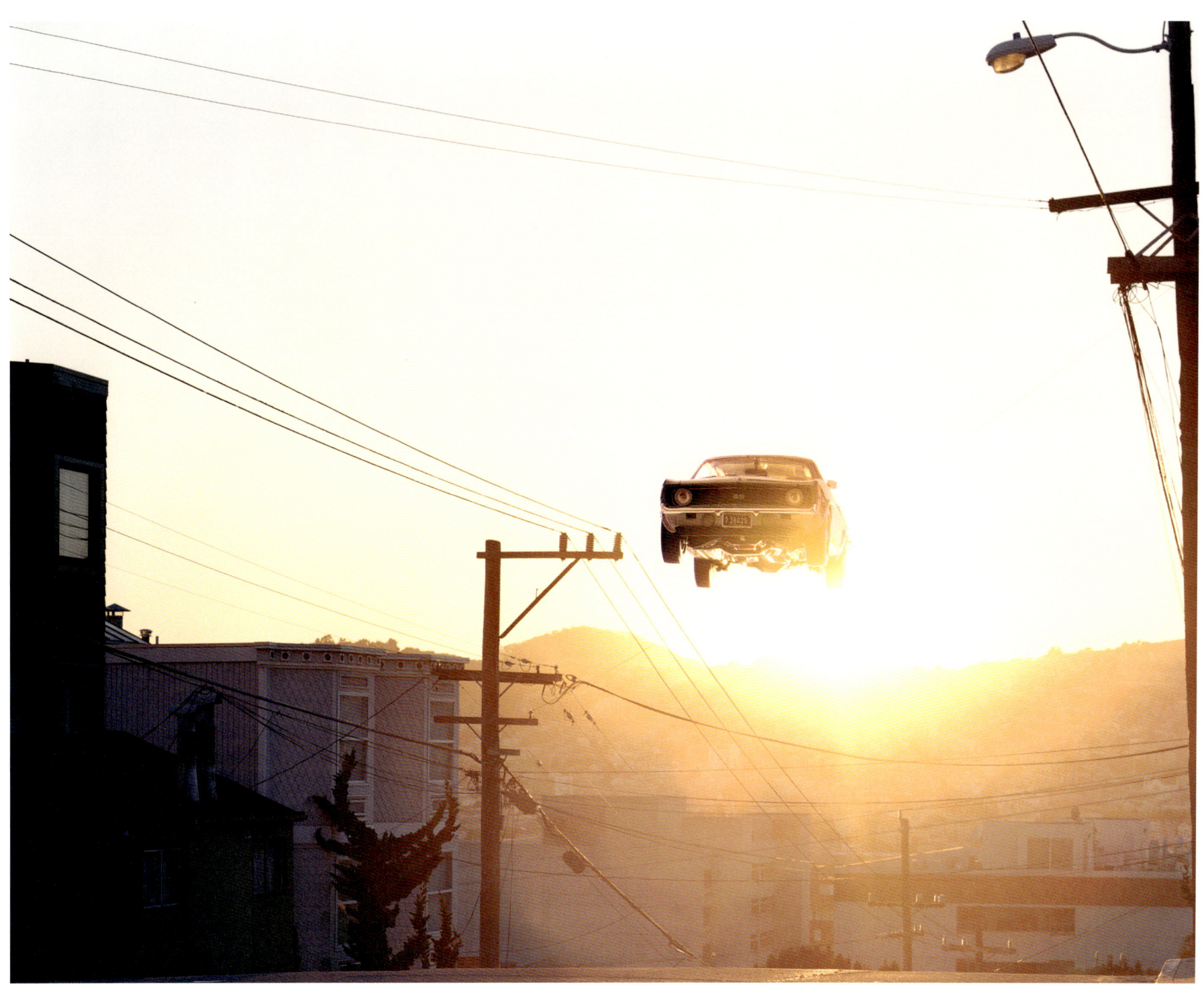

VALLEY VIEW

2013

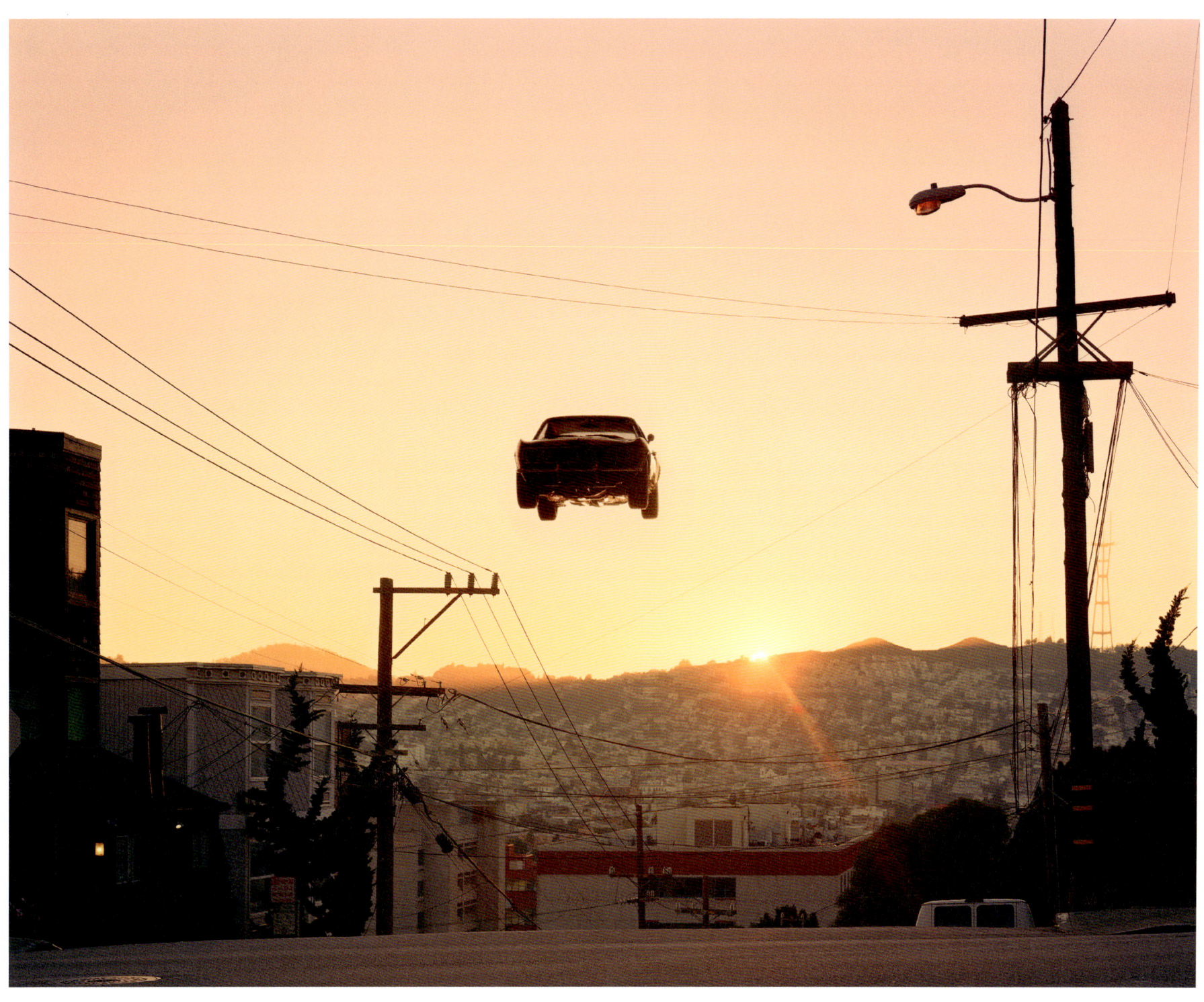

AIRPORT ROAD

2009

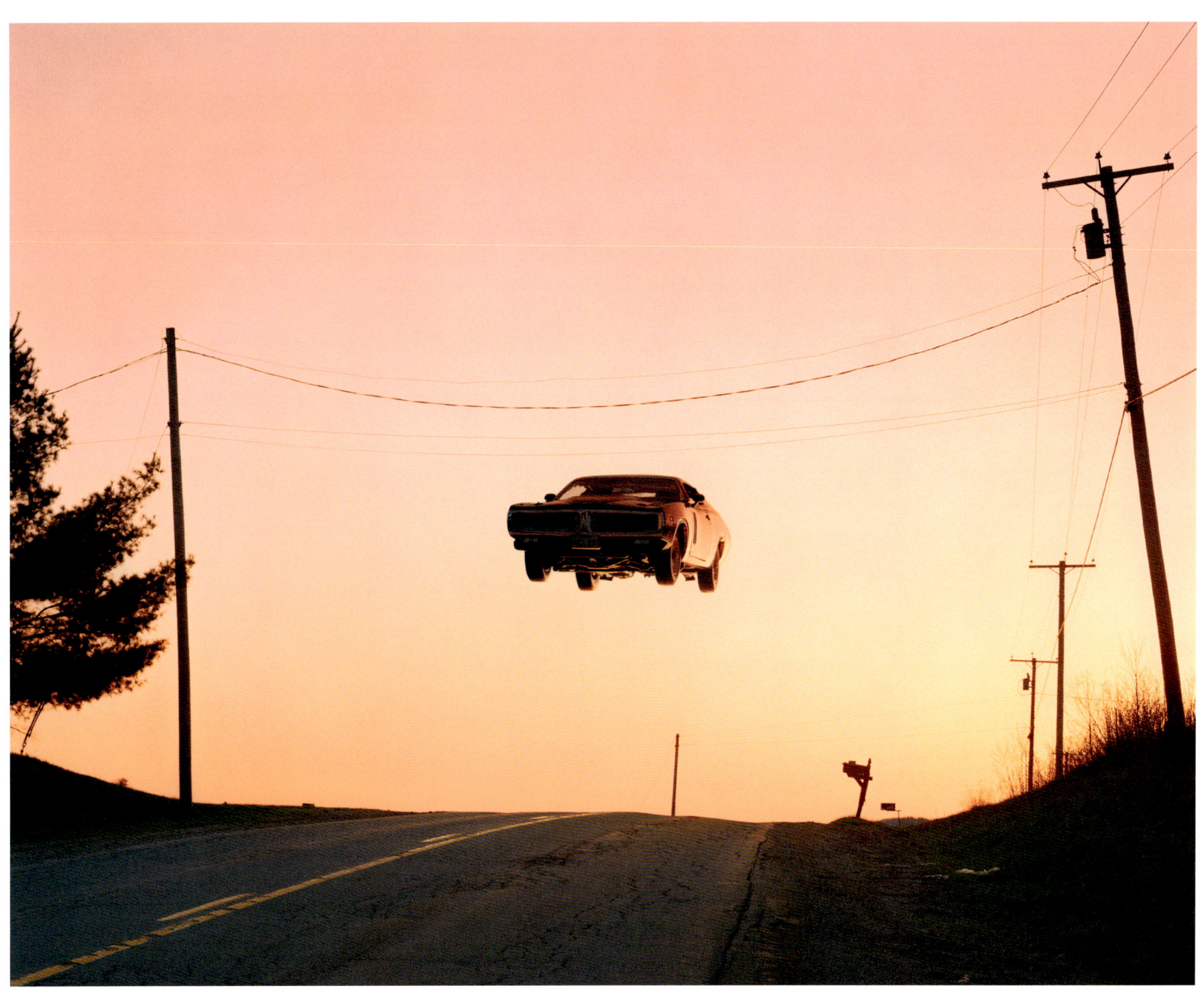

SILVER LAKE

2017

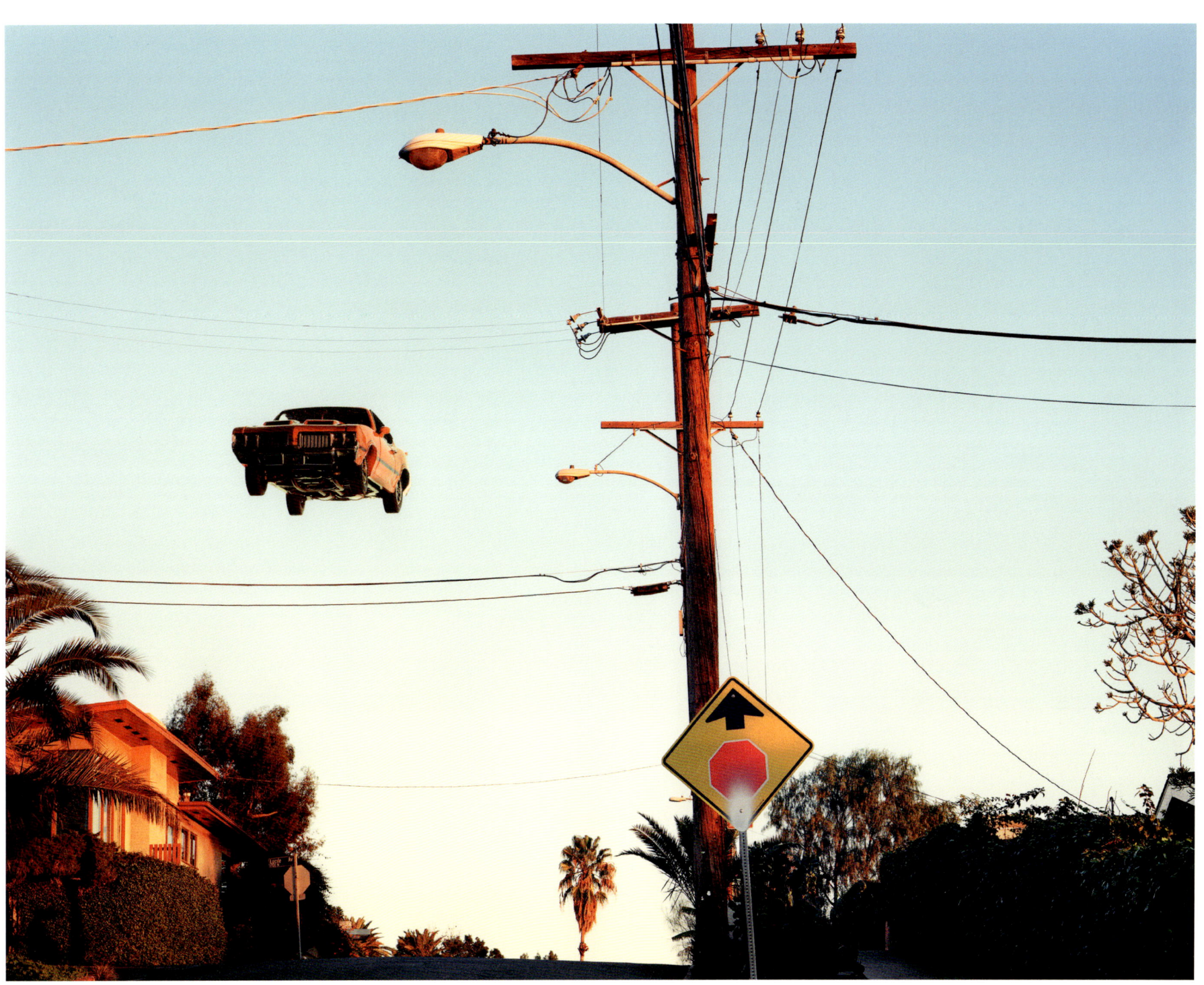

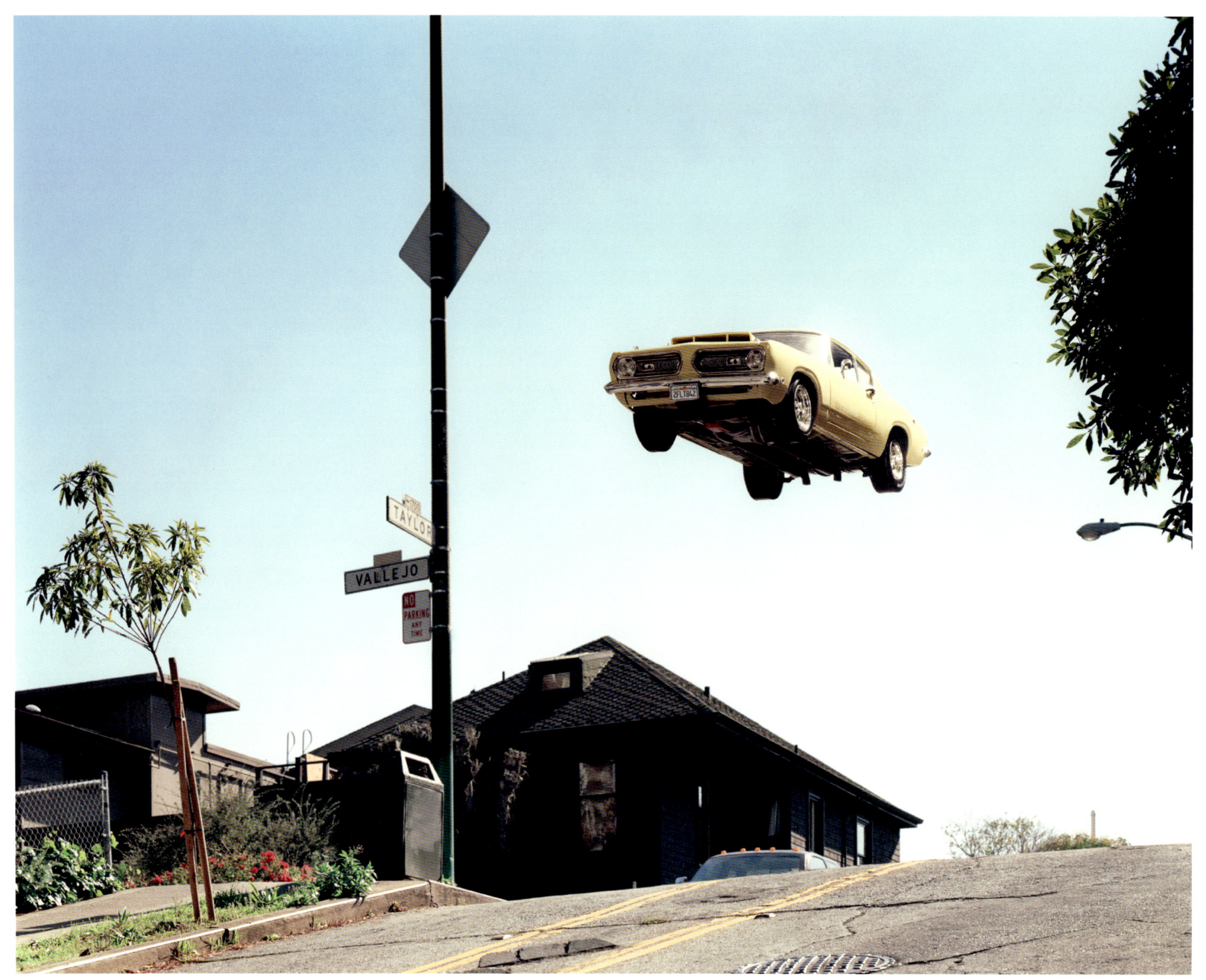

THE HEIGHTS

2006

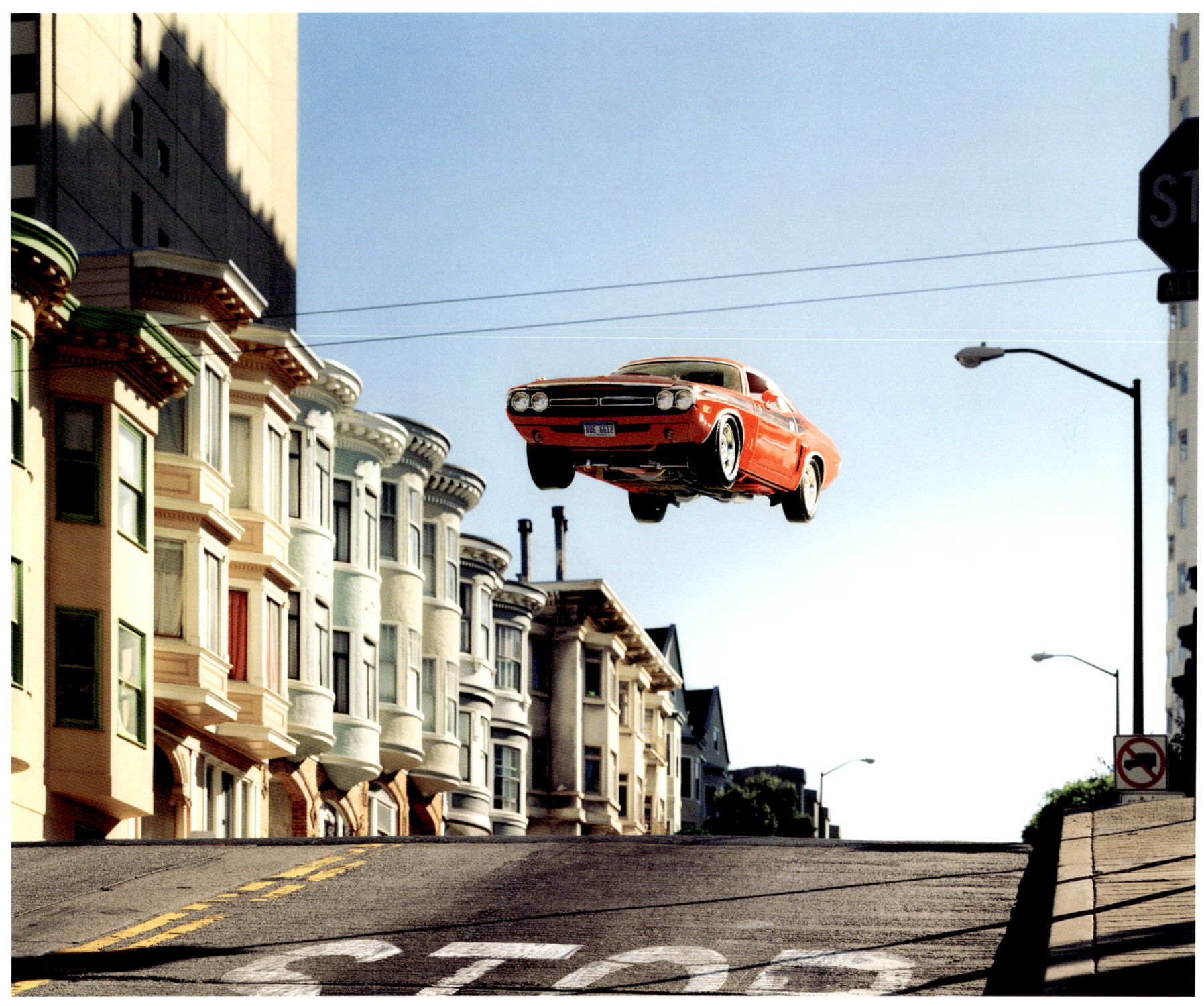

DOWNTOWN

2008

METRO CENTER

2018

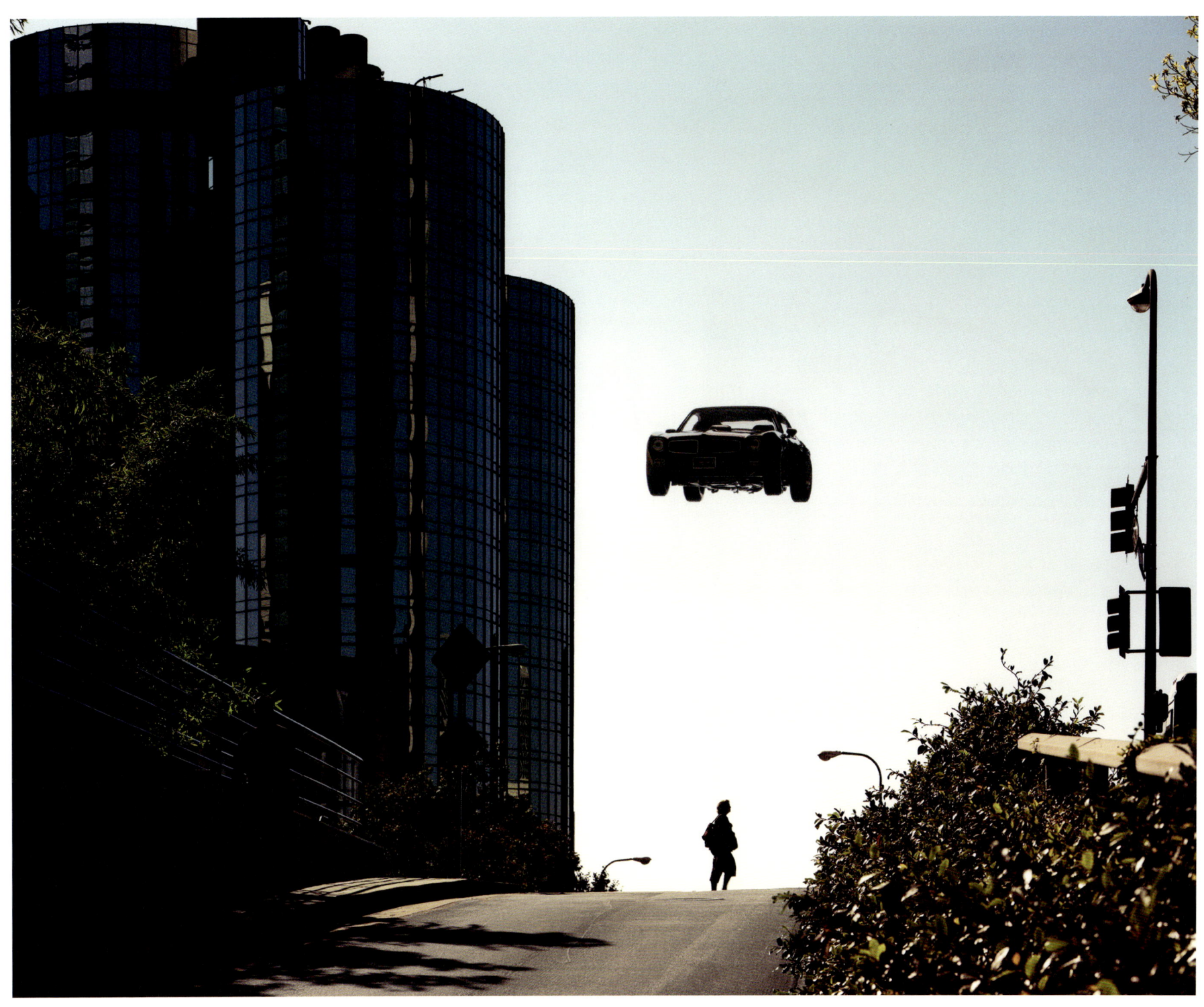

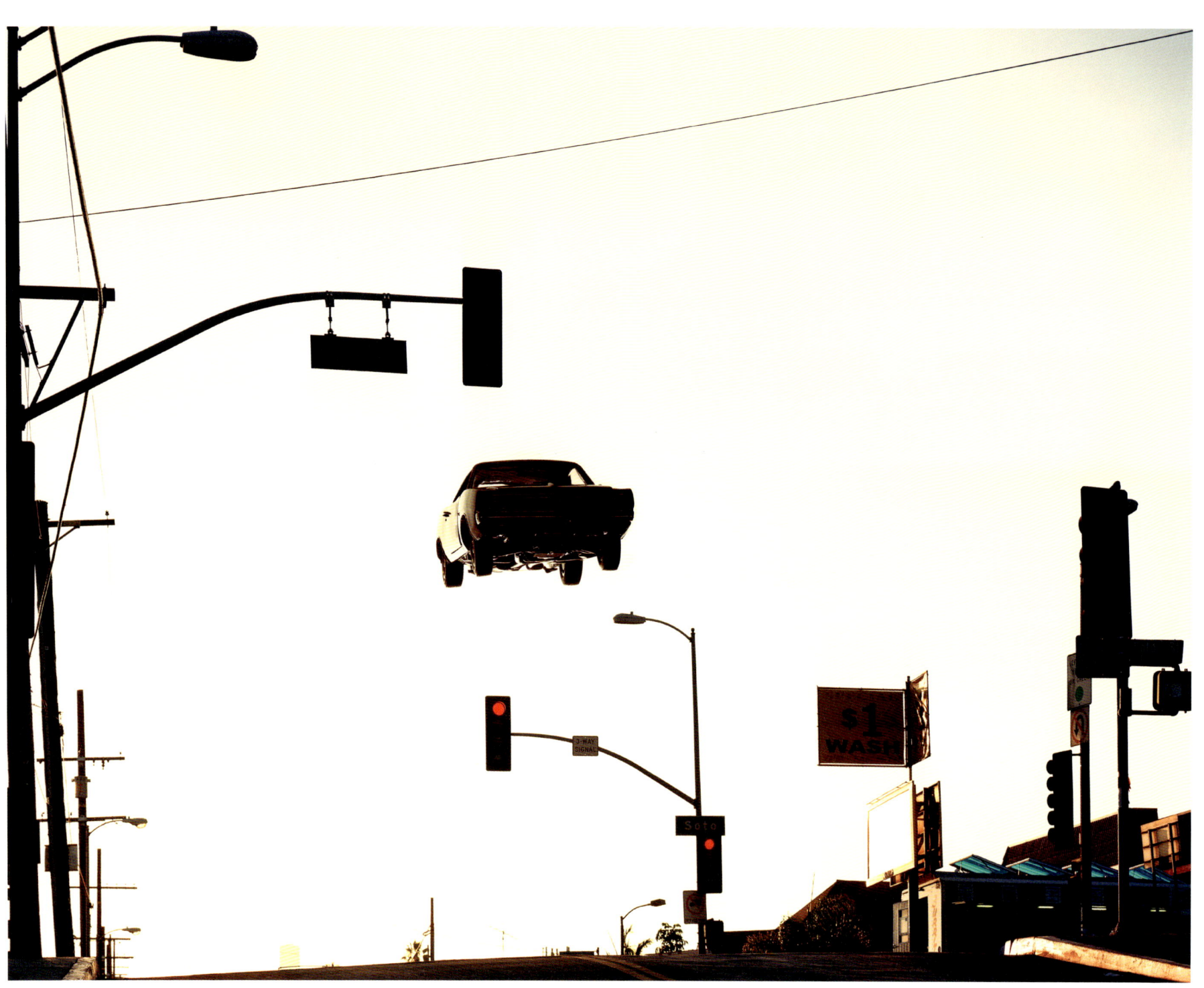

HIGHLAND PARK

2010

HYPERION

2016

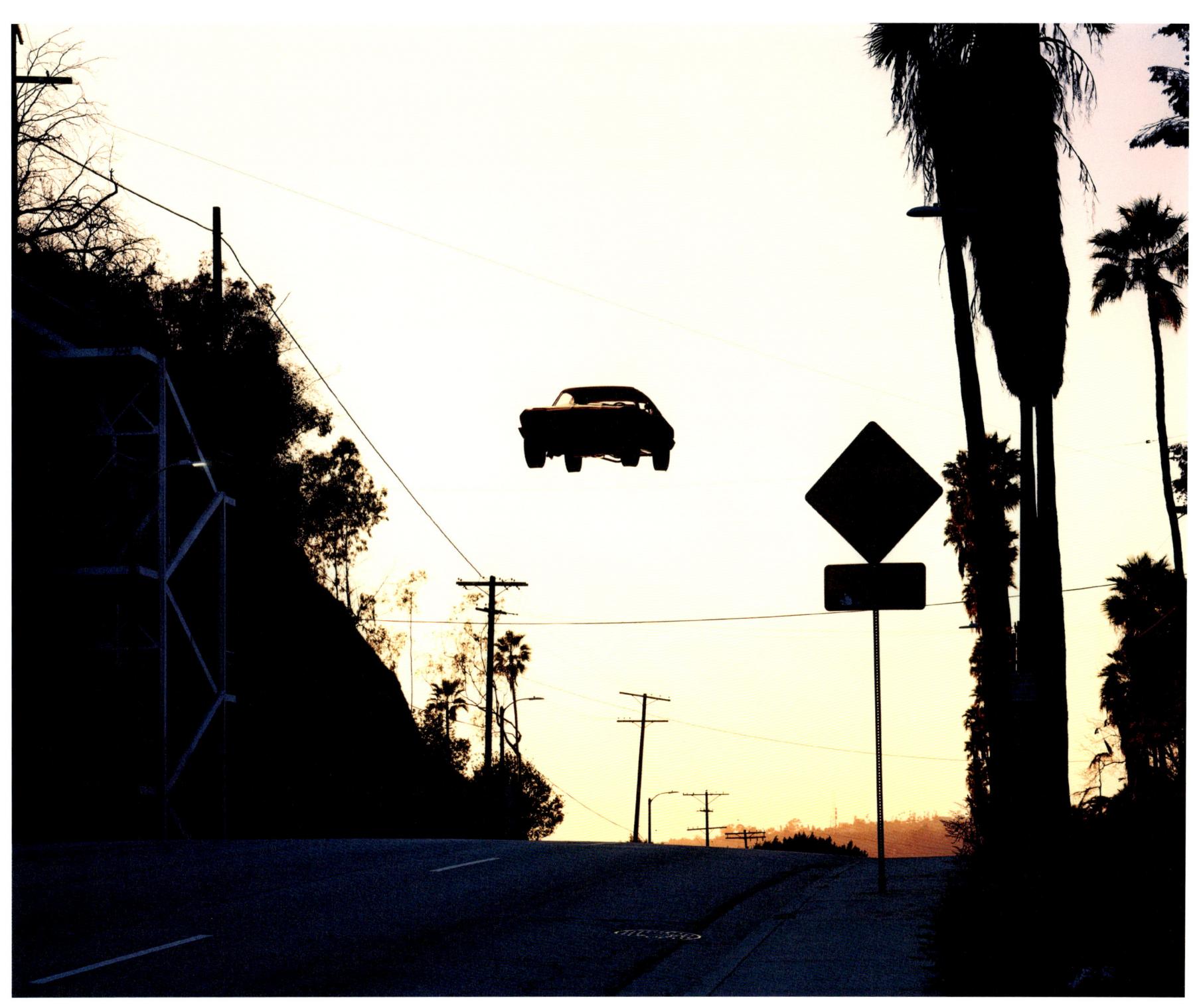

SKYLINE VISTA

2014

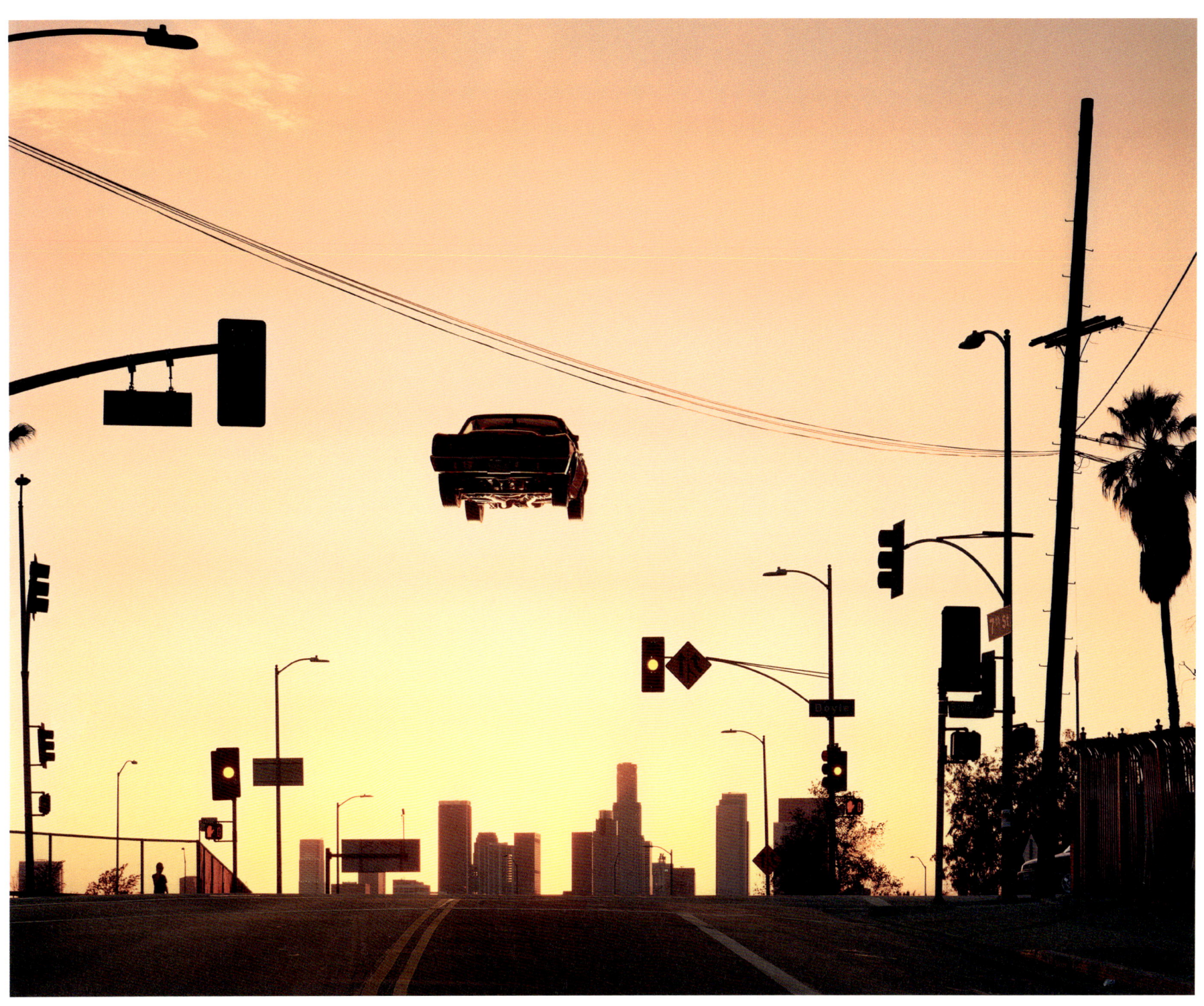

EAST SIDE
2013

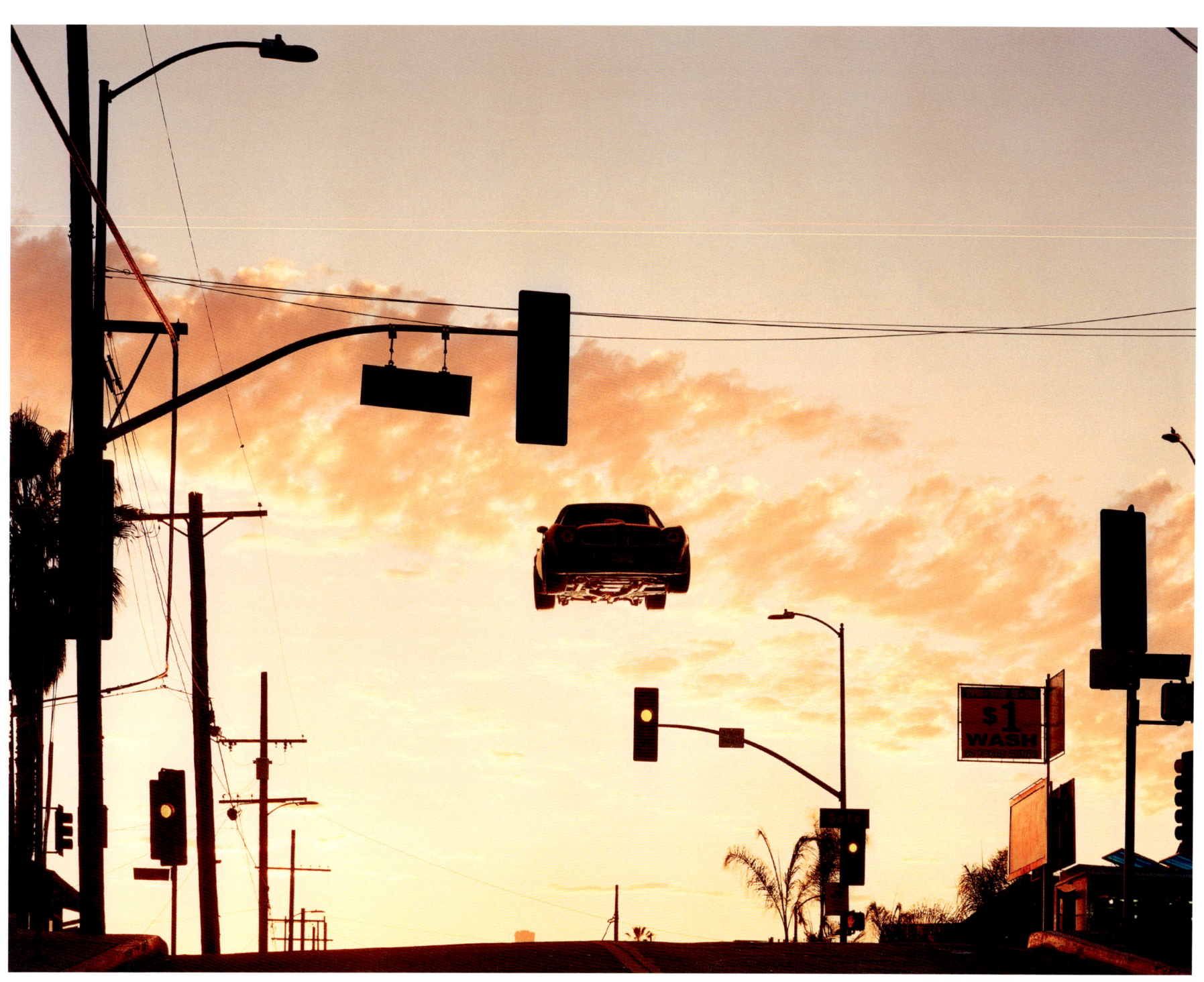

SUNSET BOULEVARD

2016

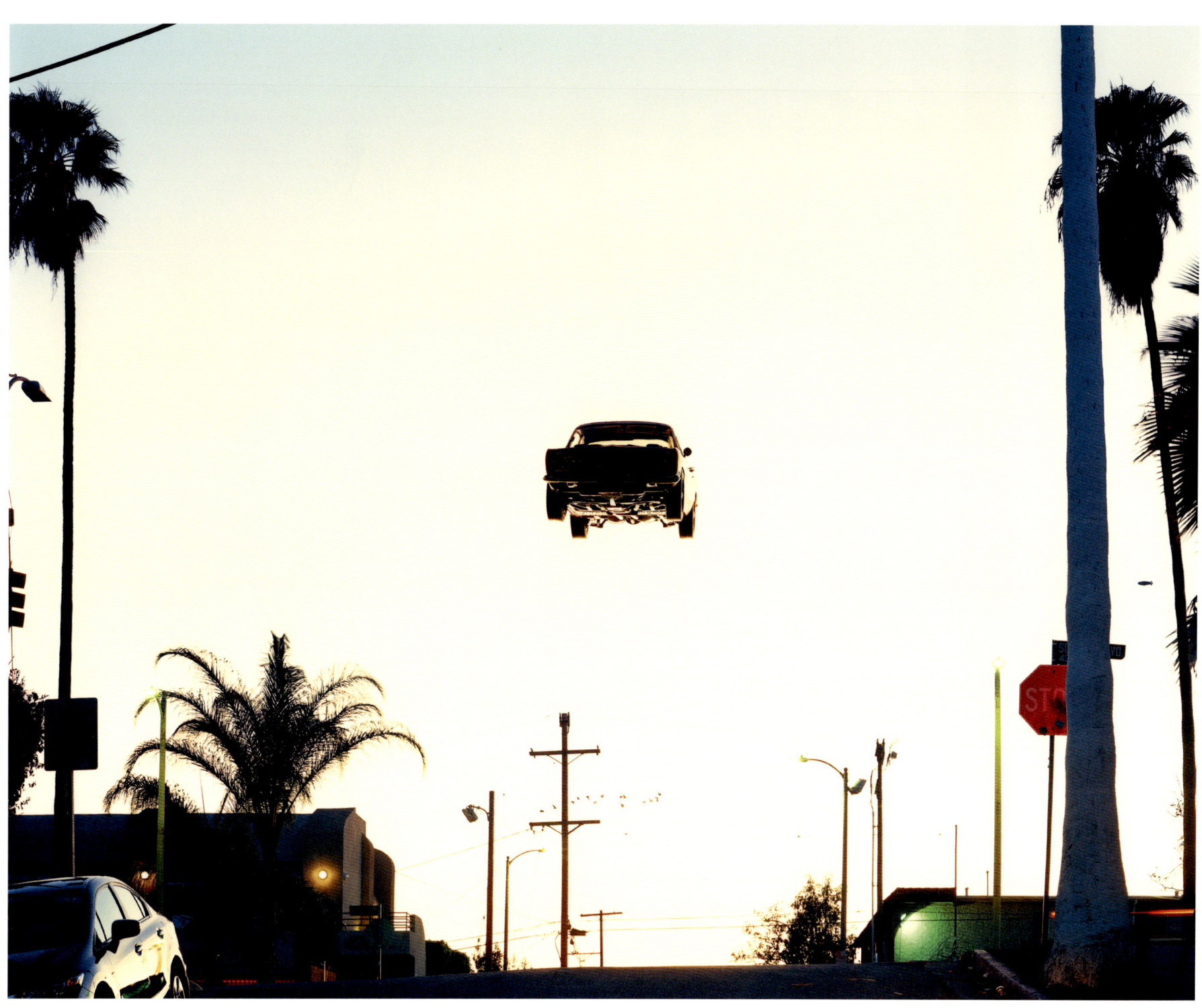

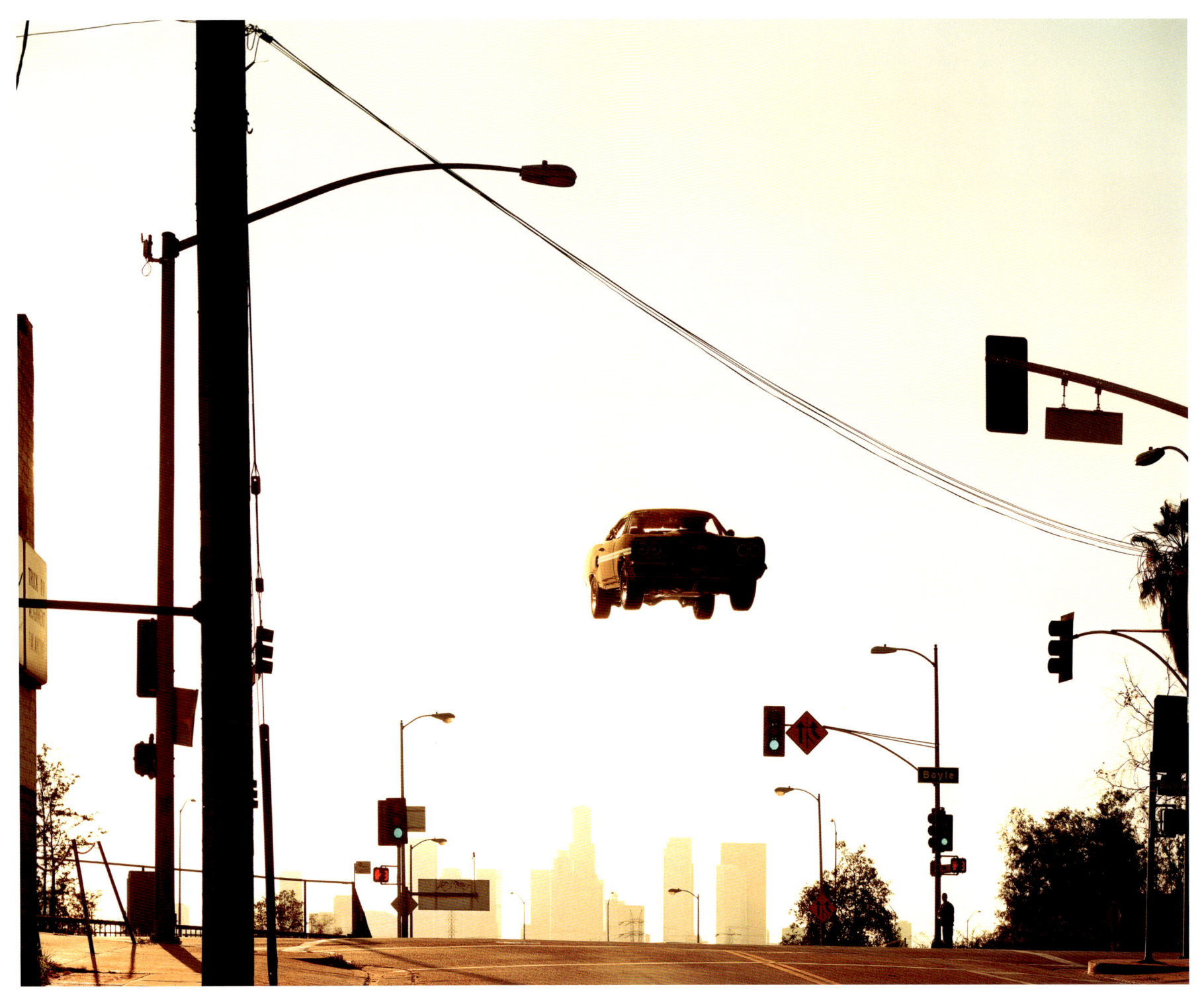

110 JUNCTION

2010

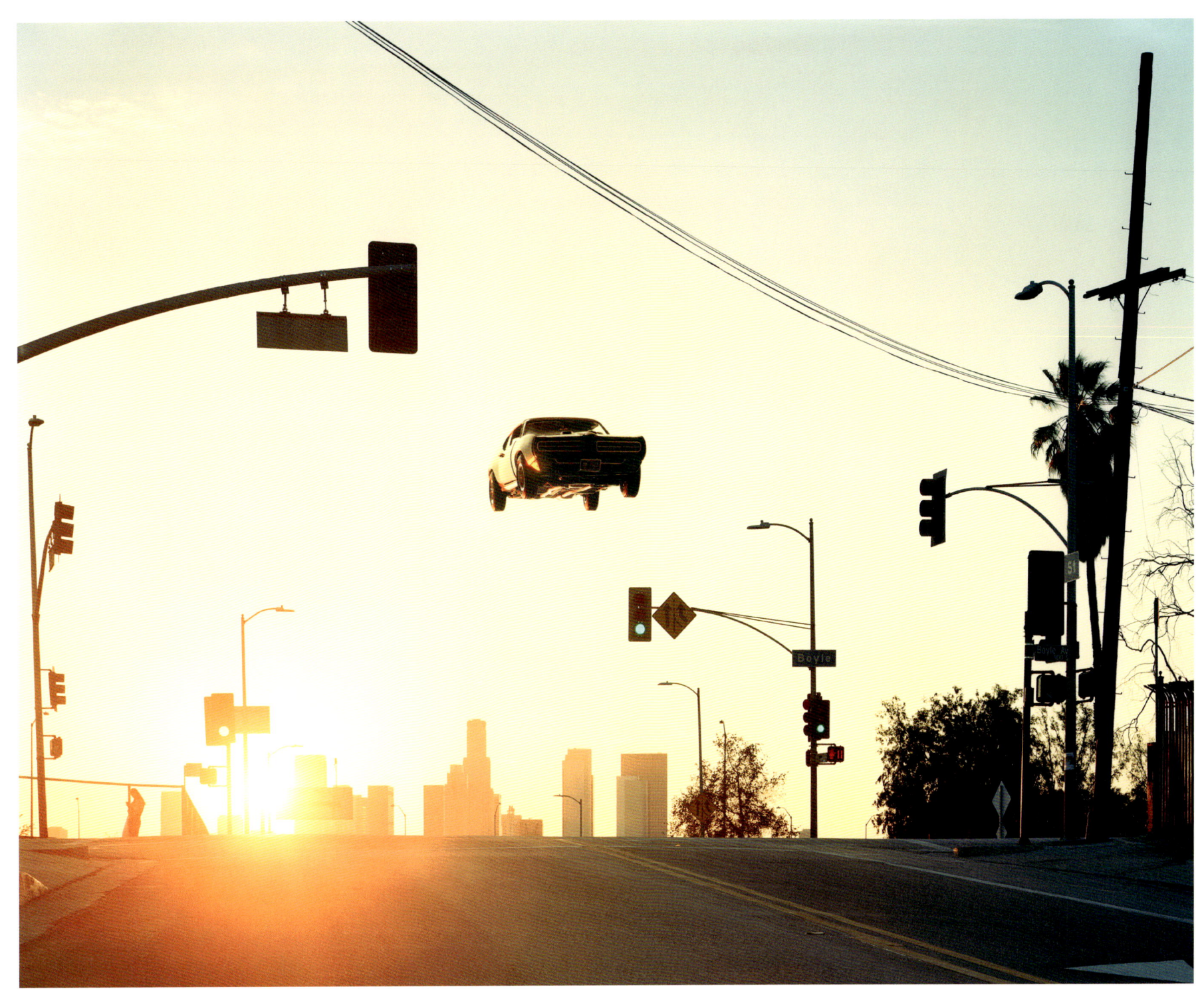

GOLD HILL

2015

BLUE RIDGE PARKWAY
2008

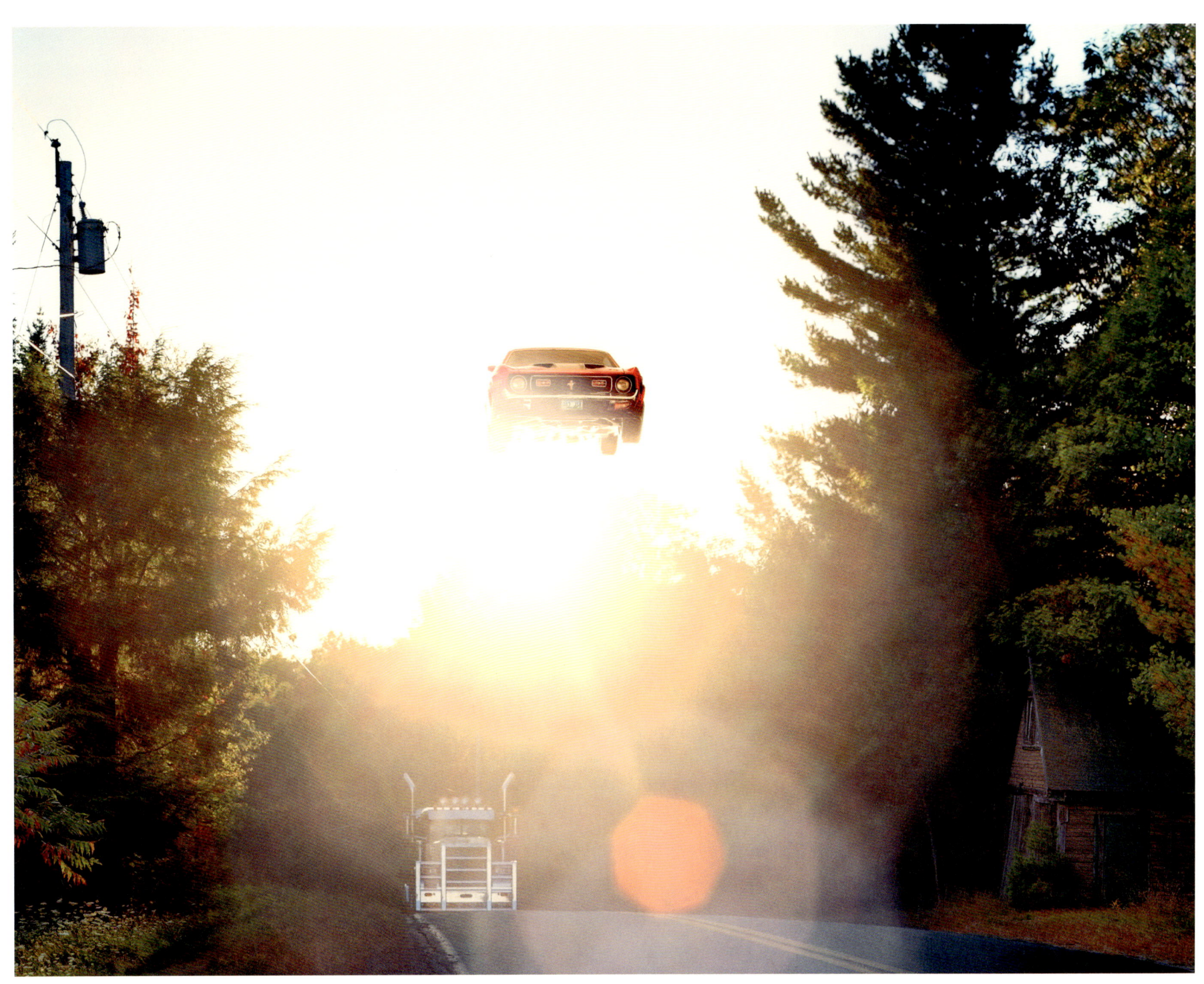

SOUTH CITY

2018

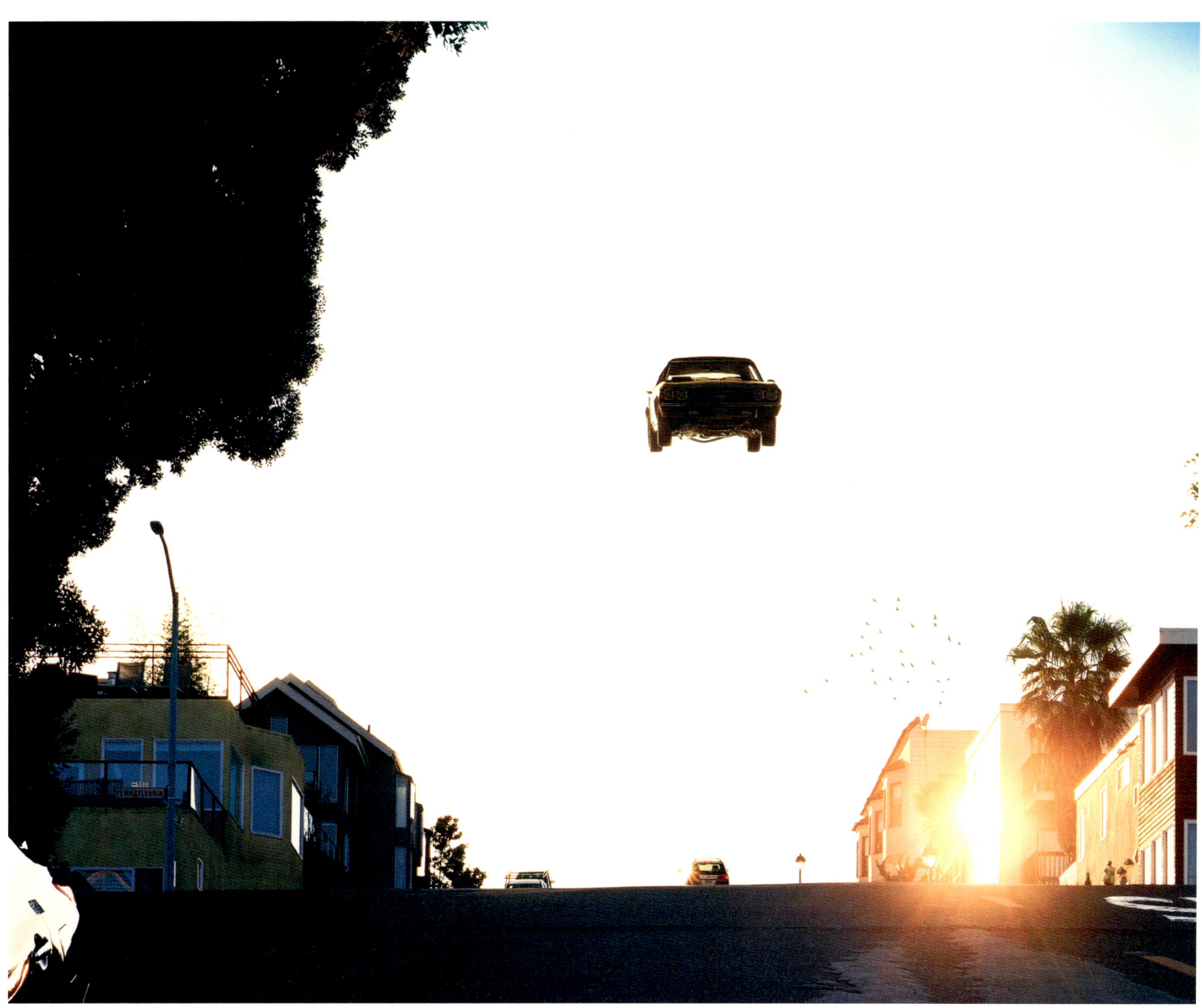

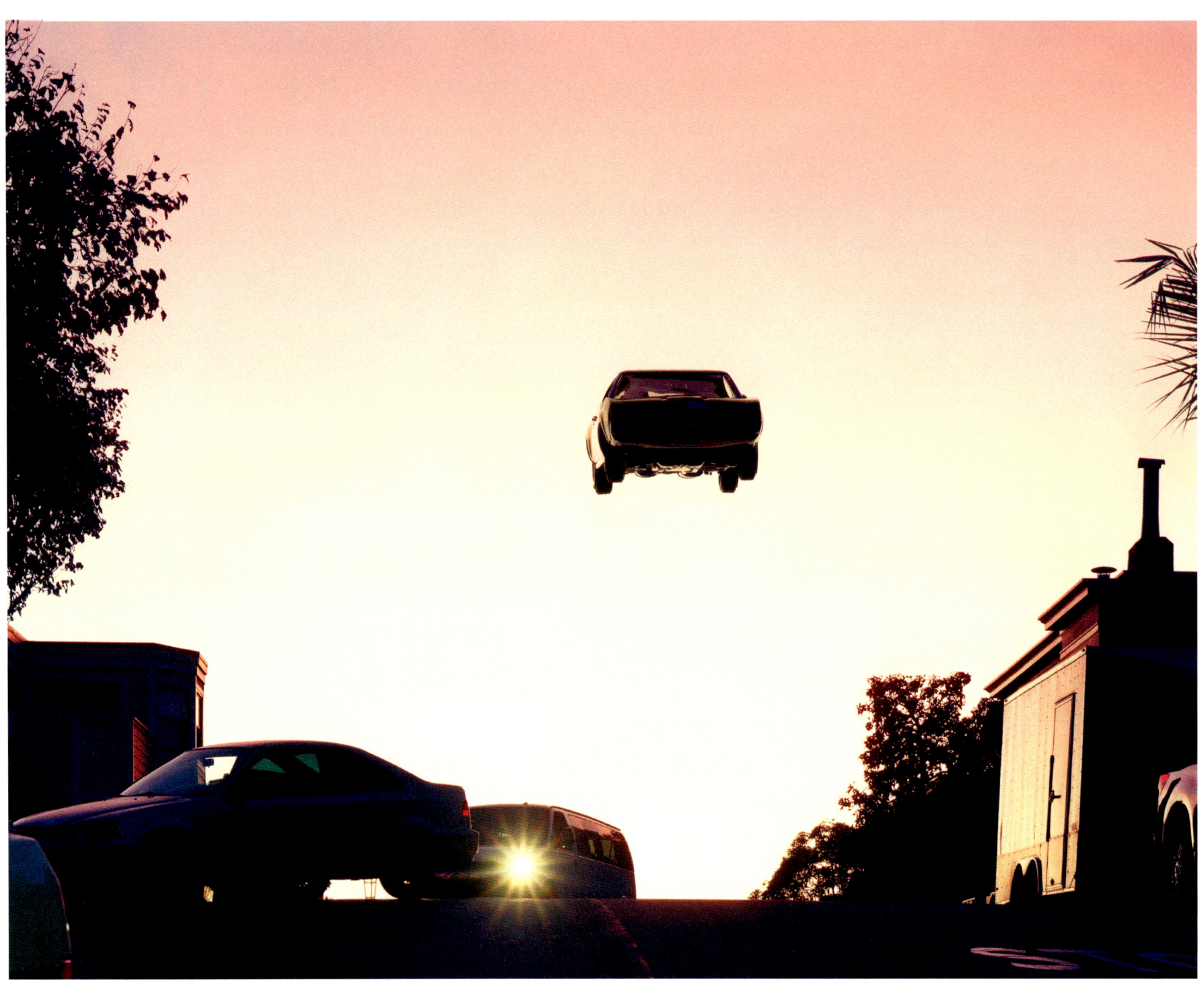

BILLY GOAT HILL
2018

PACIFIC HEIGHTS

2012

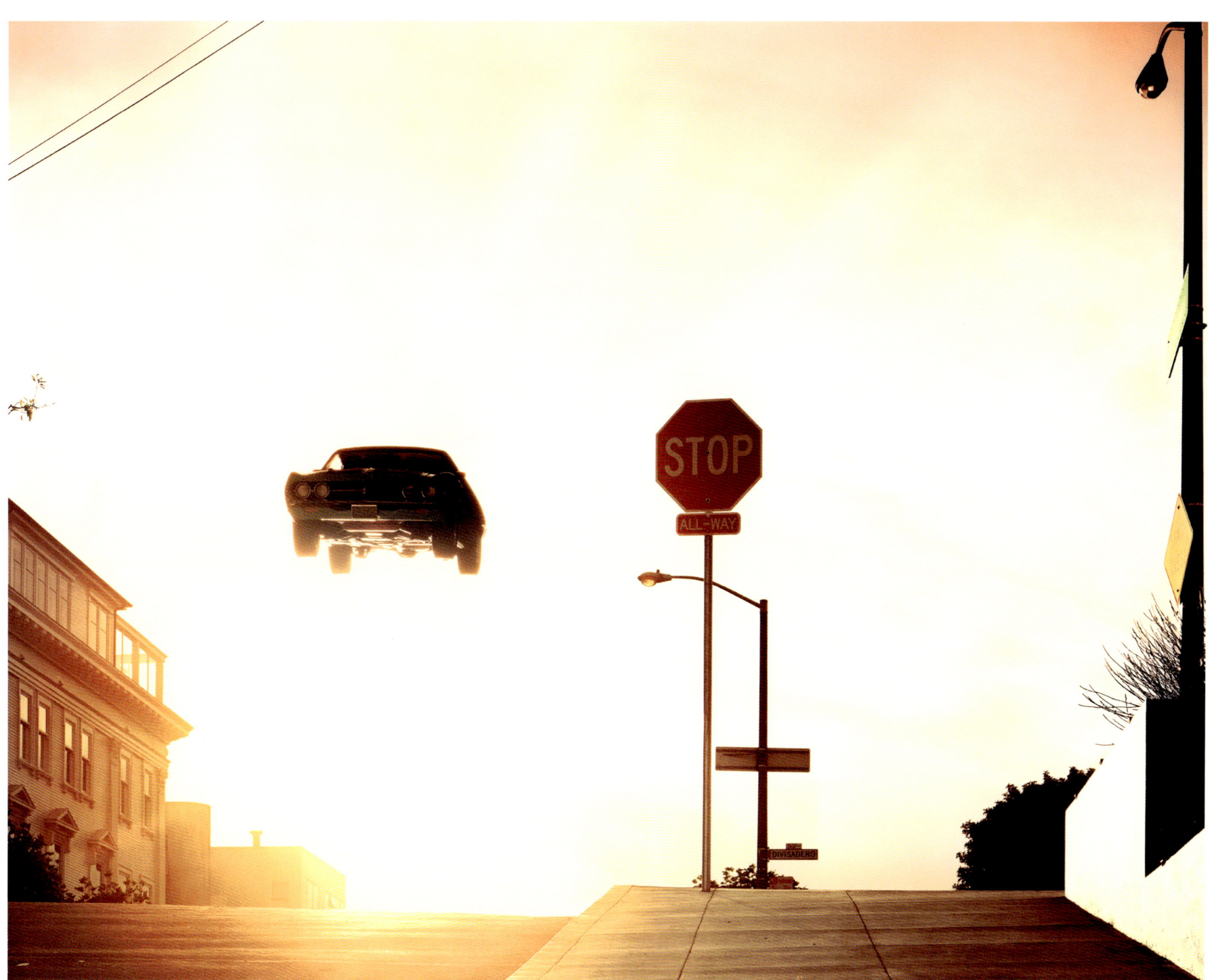

NOE VALLEY

2012

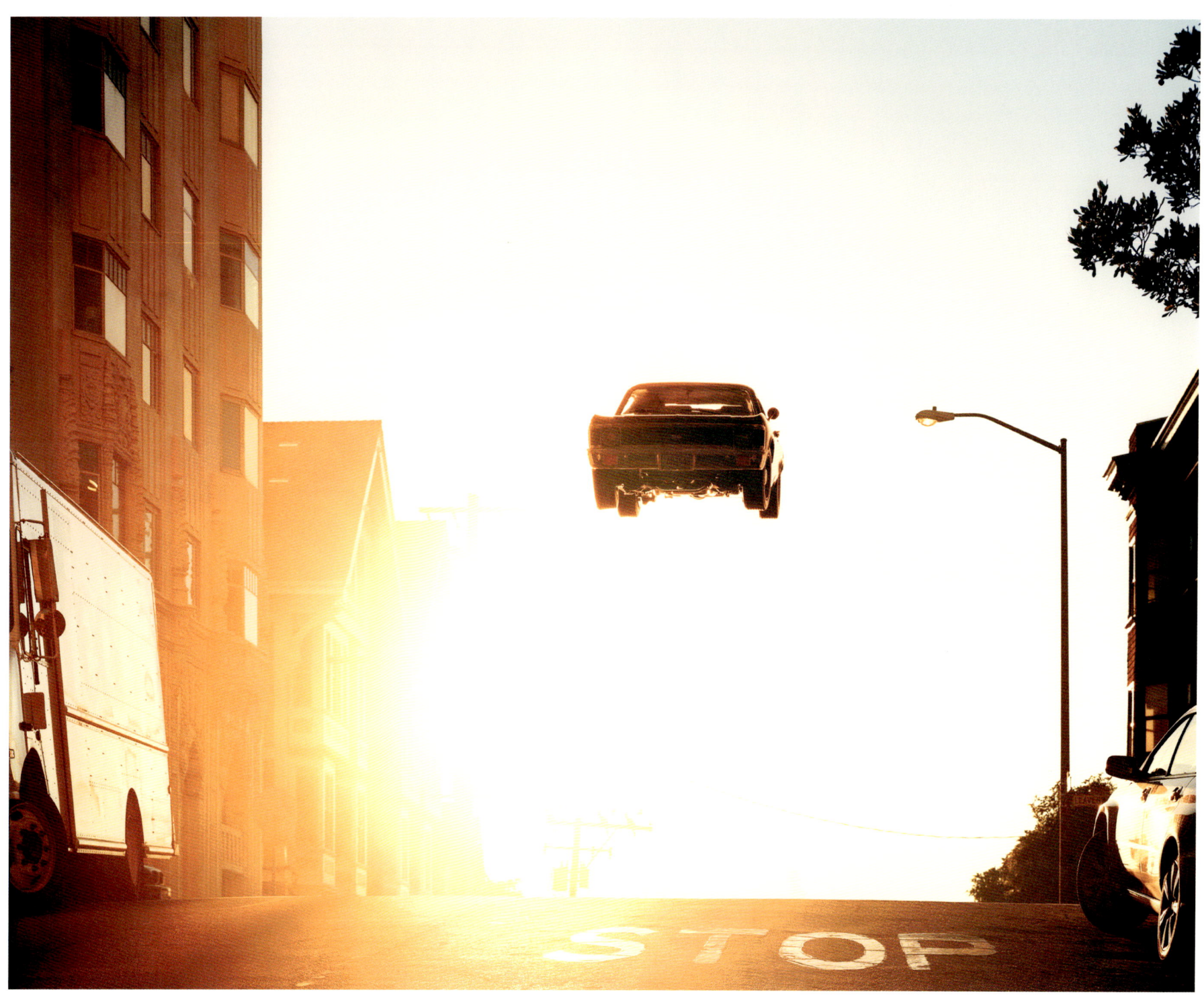

LOWER CANYON

2011

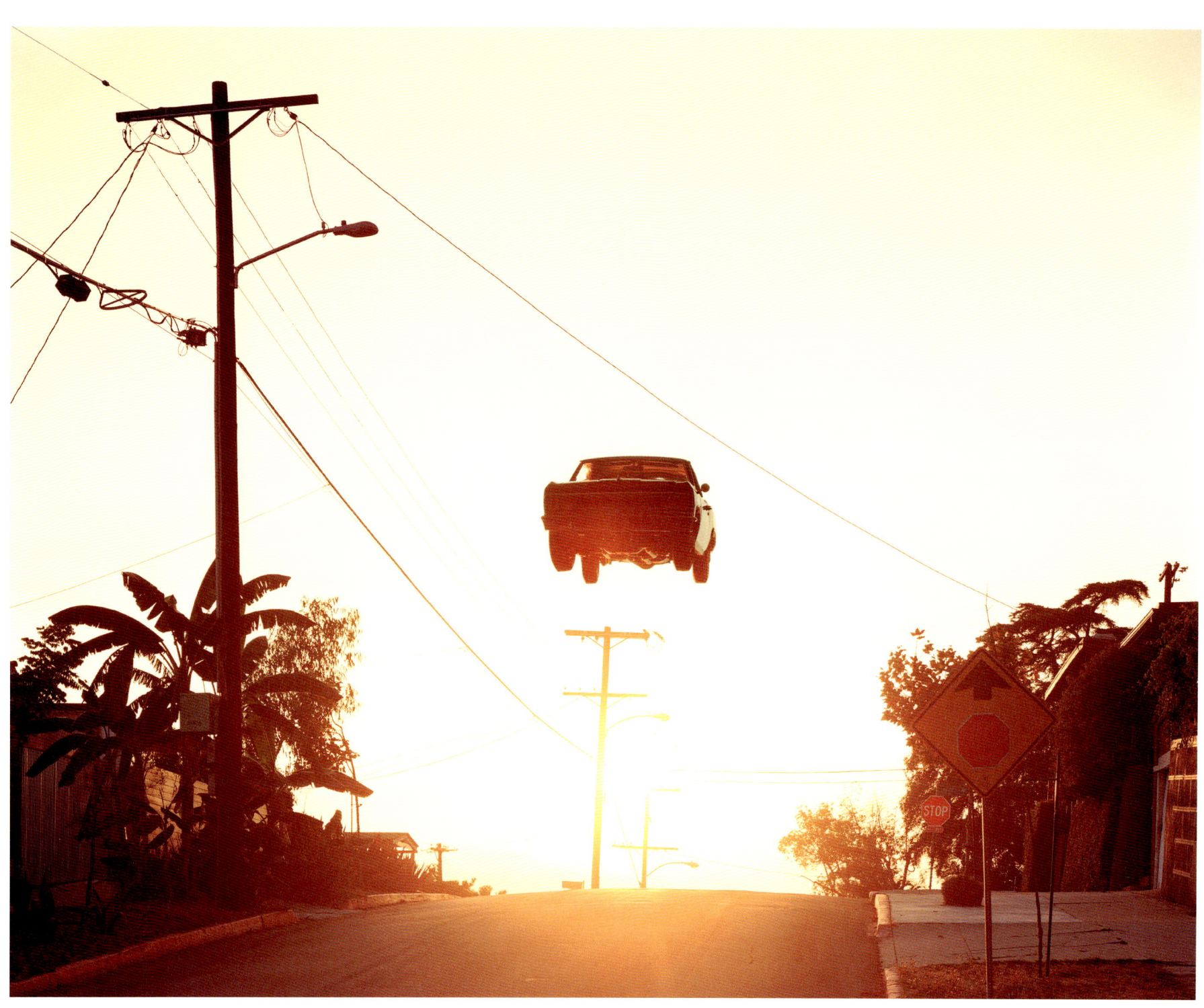

When I started this series, I was inspired by the way a car can steal the show. Iconic car chases in films are often about spectacle, and have little to do with advancing a narrative. I think of these cars as dead-end technologies—high performance machines that serve no useful function, and blatantly flaunt their own obsolescence. It seems fitting then that they remain suspended, light splashing over their lacquered hoods, reflecting the spirit and attitude of their time.

Special thanks to Lesley Martin, whose guidance and expertise are embedded in the pages of this book. Thanks to Sara Duell, who turned a desktop folder of references into a unique and thrilling cover, and Rachel Kushner, who gave poetry and substance to the subject. Many thanks to everyone at Aperture, especially Nelson Chan and Samantha Marlow. Thanks to Stephen Shore for teaching me about edges, and to Nayland Blake for making me think about the middle. I'm forever grateful to Benjamin Trigano and Shannon Richardson for taking a chance, and to Benjamin Tischer and Risa Needleman for sticking it out. Thank you, Steven Pranica, for your long-standing support. Thank you to my family. Hannah Whitaker, I love you.

For Enzo

MATTHEW PORTER (born in State College, Pennsylvania, 1975) is a graduate of Bard College and of the ICP-Bard MFA Program in Advanced Photographic Studies, New York. His work was included in *Photography Is Magic* (Aperture, 2015), and his first book, *Archipelago*, was published in 2015. Porter's work is represented by M+B, Los Angeles; Invisible-Exports, New York; and Xippas Gallery, Paris. He lives in Brooklyn.

RACHEL KUSHNER's novel *The Mars Room* was shortlisted for the 2018 Man Booker Prize, won the Prix Médicis étranger, was a *New York Times* bestseller, and is being translated into more than twenty languages. Her previous novels, *The Flamethrowers* (2013) and *Telex from Cuba* (2008), were both finalists for the National Book Award. Kushner lives in Los Angeles.

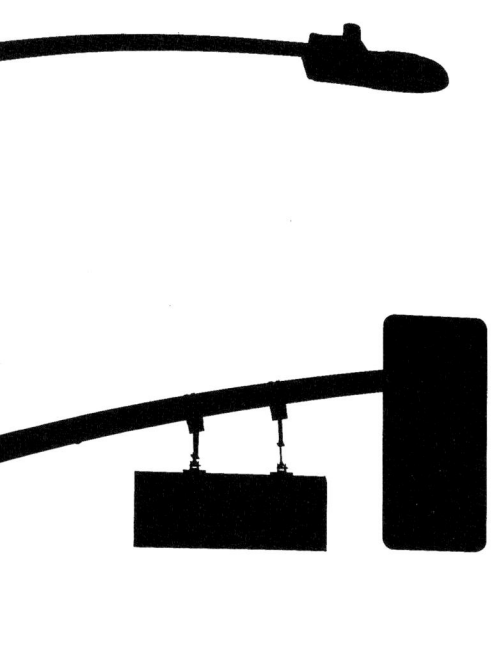

Matthew Porter: The Heights
Essay by Rachel Kushner

EDITOR: Lesley A. Martin
DESIGNER: Sara Duell
SENIOR PRODUCTION MANAGER: True Sims
PRODUCTION MANAGER: Nelson Chan
ASSOCIATE EDITOR: Samantha Marlow
SENIOR TEXT EDITOR: Susan Ciccotti
COPY EDITOR: Sally Knapp
WORK SCHOLARS: Madison Reid, Kaija Xiao

ADDITIONAL STAFF OF THE APERTURE BOOK PROGRAM INCLUDES:
Chris Boot, Executive Director; Amelia Lang, Associate Publisher; Taia Kwinter,
Managing Editor; Kellie McLaughlin, Director of Sales and Marketing; Richard
Gregg, Sales Director, Books

SPECIAL THANKS:
Matthew Porter: The Heights was made possible, in part, with generous support
from Michael Hoeh, and Kaavya Viswanathan and Joshua Lewin.

Typeset in Eskapade and Eskapade Fraktur, created by Alisa Nowak,
and Mr Eaves, created by Zuzana Licko. Custom lettering by Sara Duell.

First edition, 2019
Printed in an edition of 2,000 copies
by Artron in China
10 9 8 7 6 5 4 3 2 1

Library of Congress Control Number: 2018961499
ISBN 978-1-59711-457-8

To order Aperture books, contact:
+1 212.946.7154
orders@aperture.org

For information about Aperture trade distribution worldwide, visit:
aperture.org/distribution

aperture
APERTURE FOUNDATION
547 WEST 27TH STREET, 4TH FLOOR
NEW YORK, NY 10001
APERTURE.ORG

Aperture, a not-for-profit foundation, connects the photo community and
its audiences with the most inspiring work, the sharpest ideas, and with each
other—in print, in person, and online.